"Lois's book is filled with de
towards wanting more from n
life adversity, had me lighten up on some of my own life's challenges, and also shed a few tears of relief. I am so grateful to have
received this salve for my spirit during these crazy times."

- Jennifer Hough,
International Bestselling Author,
Executive Intuitive Coaching

"With authenticity, humour, and bravery, this memoir speaks to the
heart of every woman. Be prepared to laugh, cry, and be seen."

- Audrey Jolly, RP, OSRP, MA
author of *On The Back Of The Wildebeest*
—*The Healing Power Of Creativity.*

"Lois Lenarduzzi has one of the most invigorating voices of virtually
any writer I have witnessed. She has fun stories and powerful wisdom to spare and share. Enjoy her wonderful read."

- Elvira Hopper, Miracle Mindset Coach and Healer,
Founder of **The Love Your Vibe Transformation**
(Personal Evolution Solutions for Heart-Centred Humans.)

"I could not have read this book at a better time ... just when I have
FINALLY clued in to the pointless inner teleprompter endlessly
droning on in my head. You, Lois, have given me the gift of feeling
that I have just commiserated with a wiser sister. I will take your
advice to heart, as I too aim to envision and attain a higher aspect
of myself. I know I am not alone in this quest, and to feel your insane
but also realistic positivity in pursuing this goal are the rewards I
take with me after reading your book. Thank you. Carpe Diem."

- Louise Pitre, Actress, Singer

"Prepare for an exhilarating journey through the vivid tapestry of
life with Lois as your guide. In her captivating memoir, she effort-
lessly transforms the past into a kaleidoscope of vibrant hues,
infusing each memory with authenticity and charm. *Eat Your Crusts*

is a refreshing oasis in the literary landscape, offering a magnificent portrayal of resilience and triumph. With every turn of the page, you'll find yourself immersed in a whirlwind of emotions—laughter, tears, and unwavering belief in the power of the human spirit. Lois reminds us that age is just a number, and the journey to living life to the fullest knows no bounds. This book is a must-read for anyone seeking inspiration and affirmation that they, too, can conquer any obstacle in their path."

- Denise Marek, Award-Winning Speaker,
Author of *CALM for Moms: Worry Less in Four Simple Steps*,
Creator of the **CALM ™ Methodology for Worry-Free Living.**

"I just read Lois's book and I'm breathless, speechless, and empassioned (new word) for life. Not only is her writing easy and engaging to read, but she takes you on her perilous, outrageous, inspiring, alluring, unbelievable life journey with her. I found myself enraged at one moment, then shocked, and then laughing the next. This word, "empassioned" is inspired by who Lois is. There were many moments she shares about when other people would have given up ... totally given up. But not Lois. No matter what, Lois kept showing up. Her way of being caused positive ripples whenever she was with doctors, nurses, specialists, unhelpful people, family and friends. After reading her book, I feel alive with life—Empassioned. I highly recommend reading *Eat Your Crusts* for everyone."

- Leanne Babcock, Transitional Coach,
Best-Selling Author

"Lois is funny, quirky, and has a keen ability to make the ordinary, extraordinary, and hilarious. To me, this is the true sign of a comedic genius or, at the very least, a human being on the edge who shouldn't be allowed sharp objects. All joking aside, Lois, bravo! You should be very proud of this accomplishment.

- Judy Croon, Canada's Keynote Humourist,
Motivational Speaker, Comedian, Author,
and Stand-Up Coach at **Second City, Judy.Croon.com**

"Reading Lois's book is like time spent with the irreverent friend everyone needs in their life. She offers inspiration with a healthy dose of sass. She models the power of being totally yourself. She will lift your spirits and convince you that, yes, you need to follow your creative dreams. Anything else is not an option."

- Aprille Janes, Artist, Writer

"*Eat Your Crusts—Life Lines and Laugh Lines Of A Sweetly Warped Woman*—by Lois Howard Lenarduzzi, feels like sitting down with a good friend who knows just how to make you laugh while tugging at your heartstrings. The stories are raw, real, and filled with moments of pure courage and sass. Lois doesn't shy away from sharing the ups and downs of life, and it's this honesty that makes the book so relatable and inspiring. You'll find yourself cheering, crying, and laughing out loud. If you're looking for a book that feels like a warm, comforting hug with a side of real-life grit, this is the one. Trust me, you won't want to put it down!"

- Simone Usselman-Tod, **Stress Mastery and Mindset Breakthrough** Coach

"*Eat Your Crusts* is a captivating journey through the remarkable life of Lois Lenarduzzi. With raw honesty and vivid storytelling, Lois invites us into her world, sharing experiences that are both deeply personal and universally relatable. Each chapter is a testament to resilience, growth, and the power of the human spirit. This memoir is not just a collection of memories but a profound narrative that will resonate with anyone seeking inspiration and understanding. A must-read for those who appreciate the beauty of life's ups and downs."

- Brooke Yantzi, Founder of **Dance Alchemy,** Intuitive Coach, Speaker

Remember "Who
You Are!

Love Lois

2024

Eat Your Crusts

Life Lines and Laugh Lines of
a Sweetly Warped Woman

BY

LOIS HOWARD LENARDUZZI

STONE'S THROW
PUBLICATIONS

Cover design by Sue Reynolds
Photo by Lois Howard Lenarduzzi
Interior design: Sue Reynolds, Piquant Productions

Published by:
Stones' Throw Publications
13240 Mast Rd., Port Perry, ON L9L 1B5

ISBN: PPBK: 978-1-987813-93-7
ISBN: E-BOOK: 978-1-987813-99-9

Printed and bound in Canada

1 2 3 4 5 6 7 8 9 10

Table of Contents

Dedication

This book is dedicated to those I love, cherish and adore: my dear husband, John, and his family, my five, also sweetly warped brothers—Mike, Steve, Phil, Jeff, and Darren—and the treasure trove of gal pals with whom I have the honour and privilege to share my life. Thank you for all the laughter and tears over the years.

Foreword

I stared at the blank piece of paper that taunted me from the table in front of me and felt the cool chill of discomfort pull its icy veil around me. My paint brush was clasped firmly in my left hand and several pots of paint stood guard beyond the page upon which I was supposed to create. Were they daring me to attempt an escape? Could I sneak past them quietly and avoid detection on my way out of the room?

"I'm a writer, not an artist," I squawked.

Lois Lenarduzzi, the charming evil genius behind this experience, just smiled. "Paint whatever comes up," she chirped. "You can't get this wrong!"

Lois was inviting me to explore an aspect of my being that had been tucked neatly away inside me since my Grade 5 teacher looked at the picture I had painted and laughed shrilly at how terrible it was. I was not born with an innate ability to paint, although I'm pretty handy with a keyboard. In my own harsh opinion, even my stick figures look like chicken scratch. And nothing in my history has ever encouraged me to "paint whatever comes up." Why would I do that? And, um, HOW?

Most of my life has been about colouring inside the lines, doing what I am supposed to do, and being a responsible human being. I'm a recovering perfectionist too, which doesn't help one little bit in the pursuit of becoming "a painter." In her artistic call to action, it felt as though Lois was urging me to throw all that away and gleefully splash colours onto the page with reckless abandon!

It was an invitation to live boldly and beautifully and ignore decades of training in the pursuit of possibility. She had already shown me a selection of her own brilliant artistic creations and they had taken my breath away. But the idea of trying something like that myself, with no artistic training and even less skill, sounded dangerous.

And that's how I came to realize just how brilliant Lois Lenarduzzi is.

In sweetly nudging me into another aspect of my creative self, she was giving me permission to grow, expand, and express—to break through my own oppressive tendencies and simply give myself over to the joy of creation. And that's precisely the invitation she makes to her readers through this remarkable, beautifully written book.

Eat Your Crusts is an ode to creating an expansive, messy, and colourful life with passion, joy, and the bittersweet humility that comes from standing up again for the hundredth time after making ninety-nine face plants. The book, like Lois herself, is insightful, irreverent, unpredictable, and fun. It gives us searing reminders of the innocence that, at one point, permeated our lives.

We are Boomers, Lois and I and, at some level, we probably both aspired to the kind of squeaky-clean Brady Bunch and Partridge Family perfection that excessive television-watching programmed into us every week as children. If you're a little younger, maybe your dream life etched itself into your brain through shows like Full House or That '70s Show. Funny thing, Real Life didn't turn out that way, and we grew up anyway.

Lois is a champion of growth, and in this book, she has traced her path to shedding fears, questioning authority, and forgiving the people in her life who have wronged her, intentionally and otherwise. She brings a tender understanding to this circus called Life and dares her readers to tame the parts of it we can control—like our attitude—while walking nobly through the parts we can't—like an unwelcomed and devastating illness. Lois is a Lady Warrior who tangos with the beast of uncertainty while shovelling the coal of sad memories into the furnace of transformation so she can marvel at the sparkly rainbow smoke that results—all while wearing a cheeky grin and an awesome pair of shoes.

In *Eat Your Crusts*, she is giving those of us who want to do likewise, a playbook of sorts, that encourages us to cross the bridge to the thriving way of being in the world we desire. This is a way of "being" she has so steadfastly created in her own life, despite the curveballs and banana peels Life has so nonchalantly tossed her way.

In this book, Lois double-dog dares us to remember who we are: beautiful, powerful, creative human beings who are able to navigate the potholes in Life with dedication, grace, humour, and wisdom. She shares her stories that will bring you to tears in one moment, and make you laugh your guts out in the next. Above all, she encourages her readers to be kind to themselves, and to stop using rules and systems to "figure life out." Instead, she encourages us to dance with what presents in our own weird and oh-so-wonderful ways.

After reading this book, Lois's influence will guide you to con-firm both your own radiance, as well as relinquish the stories you have been unintentionally using to muffle your own joy. Lois re-minds us that life doesn't have to be a grease-lined slippery slope to misery. It can be an exhilarating zipline to personal mastery that catapults us through the canopy of delight, at least as often as it zooms us through the undergrowth of courage.

It took me about half an hour to find the nerve to dip my paintbrush into one of the pots of paint Lois had put in front of me. A blank page can be a terrifying companion, but I tentatively took that brush and stroked the page with first one splash of colour, and then another. Lois encouraged, praised, and supported me throughout the exercise. Where I had experienced ridicule and judgement in the past, I was now shown acceptance and validation. Under her gentle wings that day, I gained the confidence to create. The picture that resulted will never hang in a gallery or museum, and I doubt anybody will ever point to it as an example of "good art," but I enjoyed the process of creating it. And I felt good about the results.

I urge you to read this book with an open mind, and more im-portantly, an open heart. Hear Lois's stories with an eye on your own inner truths and let her wisdom settle around you as you face whatever is going on in your own life. And then, when the crusts of life are eyeing you balefully from the plate that's been put in front of you, well, you'll know exactly what to do with them.

In Joy and Gratitude,

Susan Crossman

Founder of The Awakening Author
www.awakeningauthor.com

Comely Vintage Classic
—Rare Find

A once-in-a-lifetime opportunity coming this Saturday at 10:00 a.m. Private sale with items going to the highest bidder through Sassabies Auction House. Previewing top-of-the-line inventory on-ly. All sales are final, and items come with papers of authenticity.

Item # 333

This lovely piece is to be enjoyed for years to come. Slight in scale and size, with lovely curves. Takes up minimal space in the home. Exterior is firm-ish, flexible and sound with some wear and tear, sagging and lagging due to overexposure to the harsh elements. Balance is somewhat askew, and therefore, stands a tad off-kilter, adding to its unique mid-century charm.

Has had some major reconstruction in the past, resulting in a few hitches and glitches, which has only made it stronger and more resilient.

This valuable piece requires the utmost care—opportunities for creative expression, naps, blankies, good books, foot rubs, hikes, dancing, chippies, and lots of hugs, kisses, and affection. Frequent emotional cleansing and purging is an absolute must to maintain its inner sanctum. Also, please note—prefers heat over cold. Very important.

This fine specimen also demands solitude in high doses, mixed with exposure to nature, community, and great friends. Wild and crazy, fun-lovin' and high livin' is mandatory to keep this gift to the

1

human race in fine running form.

It's well worth the investment, time, and effort as its attributes speak for themselves ... kind, generous, sensitive, compassionate, assertive, intelligent, and courageous. Now top this off with a sweetly warped sense of humour and you've got yourself a treasure to behold.

Nothing is perfect, so we would be remiss if we didn't mention a few dents in the fender. It likes to get its own way, interrupts people when they are speaking, can be sarcastic, spoiled, bratty, fussy, bossy, judgey and has been known to have a sharp tongue. This precious gem is totally worth the stress, headaches, and frustration of owning a determined, headstrong seeker of "the way, the truth, and the light."

Ladies and gentlemen, this genuine article could be yours for a fraction of its total worth. Don't hesitate, now's your chance; don't miss out.

Look for the exhibit on the second floor entitled, "Goddess of Sobriquet," also known as (AKA) Lo, Lojo, LoLo, YoYo, Oolith, Lo-Ass, Blowis, Floiss, Lo-ee, Stumpy, or Lola.

Introduction

A close friend of mine wrote this note to me well before this book was written. It said, "You are the most inspiring woman I know, my LoLo, so get your pen moving and share your stories with all of us so that some of that wisdom, vulnerability, and love seeps from the pages into our hearts. Thanks for doing this for all of us." These words were a call-out to the writer in me to "stop thinking about it and do it, dammit."

My dear readers, after almost two years of sifting, mixing, and assembling, my latest creation is now warm and ready from the literary oven to be chewed on and savoured. Hope you enjoy it!

I was one of those kids who was terrified to be called upon by the teacher to answer a question or to put my hand up to ask one. Standing up in front of a class to read aloud or make a presentation would give me the willies. I can't recall how or why this fear was born in my psyche, but it's remained buried in my subconscious mind for years. I have weaved, bobbed, and skirted this fear on many occasions in my life.

I began to face this fear by "putting myself out there" in my late thirties, early forties. *If not now, then when?* I asked myself. The shit hit the fan around this time with numerous health issues arising and I had to give up my massage therapy and yoga practice. My creativity portal opened when my business, health, and vitality closed down. While recovering from two major surgeries in two years, I decided to open the creativity toy box and try my hand at painting, even though I had no idea what the hell I was doing. After that, I decided to try my hand at writing.

In the early 2000s, I joined a creative writing class. We wrote short stories and as the members got to know each other, the writing began to go deeper into the touchy-feely stuff. When one person became vulnerable, others followed until it became the norm to witness the participants in the class moved to tears, joy, laughter, and sorrow when someone read their work out loud to the class. My earliest stories seemed sweet and safe; I wasn't yet ready to hang myself out to dry, buck naked, revealing all my inner lumpy bumps for all to see. Though, after seeing the effects of "the power of the purge" on the page, it inspired me to step it up a notch.

In order to stretch the waistband of courage to make more room for more gutsiness in my writing, I started with personal stories I felt either deserved honourable mention or still held some emotional charge in my memory, making me laugh or cry. I asked myself, *Do I want to continue to hide, censor, and protect myself from other people's opinions and judgments, or do I want to earn a Brownie badge for going deep, becoming bolder and more daring in sharing not only the upbeat times, but also the shitty-shit-shit I've experienced as well?*

A few years later, knees knocking, I even talked myself into getting on stage to sing and act with absolutely no experience or training! I did this to stick my tongue out at the fear that said, "No way, no how, you can't do this." Was I good? "Compared to whom?" I ask. All I know is I "faced the dog that wanted to bite me," and was proud of my moxie and determination. Plus, I put another chit into my self-mastery deposit box. The bonus was that the four of us who made up the Rack Pack Comedy Show had a blast putting it together.

The more I challenge myself to take risks, the more I am making it loud and clear to the fraidy-cat voice inside me that I'm steering my own ship here; running into storms is just part of this fantastic voyage.

Writing this book has been scratching at the "Do it, dammit!" door for many moons. The idea felt daunting and like many writer wannabees, I thought, *Who the hell am I to write a book?* The calling wouldn't go away even though I turned my head, inserted fingers into my ears, and yelled, "La la la, I can't hear you!"

Putting pen to paper, I tip-toed gingerly into my past for a spell, then fell head-first into a dung-heap of sorrow, shame, confusion, and fear, and I came out of this creative sweat-lodge gasping for air. I dove back in, creating an even deeper connection with myself by circling in, around, and through what lives inside of me. I double-dog-dared myself to record stories that made my heart blossom, broke me down, and broke my heart, all the while growing stronger and more determined in the process. I decided I no longer wanted to play in the "have-to" world of living up to, fitting in, gaining approval, or seeking validation.

Writing stories about my life was like pulling the curtain back and revealing the mystery behind the suffering—the programs and patterns within me that said, *I can't, no way, people will judge and criticize me. They'll think, "who does she think she is ... something special?* These were old, outdated voices in my head from childhood, passed down from generations before. Writing my truth, while charting this crazy course, was "veddy veddy skeddy," but a clever way to thumb my nose at conformity and give up the myth of, "I'm gonna get slammed." It truly was a gift to myself, from myself, for my sixty-fifth birthday and it said, "I matter. My story matters."

Everything in this memoir-ish book of mine is kinda, sorta, mostly true, except for the parts that aren't. That's to keep you guessing. Oh, just a head's up: I have written these stories in "my voice" and consequently there may be some quirky, bizarro, and questionable Lois-isms within the pages of this book. No apologies here, this is how I really talk every day in real life. Stay with me, k?

The phrase, "Eat your crusts", obviously has some significance in my life, because I chose it for the title of this book. Growing up, my dad told us he had a cousin who died from not eating his crusts. He said crusts were good for you, and I better eat them because they'd make me grow big and strong. I assume this silly anecdote went in one ear and out the other because I dug my heels in refusing to eat those nasty little suckers and left most of them on the plate like abandoned soldiers on the battlefield. We—my parents and I—fought to the finish on this one, and I won. I don't like crusts; I never have, never will. My five brothers and I still crack up when we tell this silly story to others who have contempt for crusts like I do.

Let me explain another reason why this title is significant to me: crusts are like dry toast—boring and blah. The outer layer of the bread can be tough, resistant, and hard to swallow, much like life's adversities ... loss, pain, and grief. It makes sense the more robust the crust, the more it exercises and strengthens our chops for what's to come. On the flip side, we slather butter, jam and honey all over the soft, fluffy, easy-to-chew inner part, which is much like the sweet, yummy stuff life has to offer – joy, friendship, passion, adventure, excitement, creativity, and connection. You can't have one without the other—they make up the slice of life. It is the sustenance that not only supports, nourishes, and satisfies us throughout our lifetime, but helps us grow into the person we came here to be, sturdier and more robust. I may not always like to eat the crusts, but sometimes I just can't avoid eating some of them; and neither have I avoided a few whiz-banger events in my life that turned me upside down like a turtle on his back, struggling to maintain my "normal," whatever that is. And besides, there are some crusts that are downright more palatable than others, wouldn't you agree?

My hope in sharing these stories with you, dear reader, is to entice you to do something that wows you and scares you at the same time, like sailing, singing, acting, building, travelling, flying, dancing, and even doing something as simple as changing your hair-style. It's a call to wake up, shake up, open up, and speak up with the spunk and pluck akin to that of a three-year-old. Keep your eyes peeled for those windows and doors held ajar for you to climb through so you can discover what's waiting on the other side. They're there ... really. Cross my heart.

If I can entertain, raise a few eyebrows, and maybe even inspire some tears and laughter, then I have fulfilled my purpose in writing this book. Establishing a meaningful connection with you through shared life experiences would be "all that and a bag of chips," for me, as the author. However, to do this you must first connect deeply with yourself, and that, my dear friend, is a calling that comes from within. This book is my calling. What's yours?

The Story of my Life

My family moved into our brand new, custom-built, four-bedroom split level in 1965. It was situated on top of the Niagara Escarpment, also known as (AKA) "The Mountain," in Hamilton, Ontario. Living on "The Mountain" in Steeltown was code for "you made it."

Our new digs sat on a 65 by 175-foot lot and was designed for a good-sized brood, which worked out well as there were seven of us in my family at the time—Mom, Dad, four boys and me. Three of my siblings were older than me and one was younger. Our subdivision backed onto an apple orchard on one side and Hillfield-Strathallan Private School on the other. This school was primarily for rich, smart kids. My brothers and I, however, went to Buchanan Park Public School.

The lower half of our new house was covered with barn-red and ink-black coloured brick. The upper level of the "split" was covered with wood siding painted a light-toast beige that was to require yearly up the ladder maintenance in the coming years. The front door and two garage doors were painted a "Cheezie" orange shade, like the cheese-dusted, crunchy corn snack. The colour combo would make a home designer's eyes twitch.

Mom tried to talk Daddy-o into a more muted, complimentary colour as she was a pastel gal, but he wouldn't budge. He was totally oblivious to the raised eyebrows and snickers from onlookers.

The basement was the kids' domain—home of the bright orange-flowered, booger-smeared chesterfield. Down in the dungeon, as Mom referred to it, the two older boys competed for alpha status by regularly beating the crap out of each other while Philip, brother number three, would command his little green plastic army men for hours at a time. Jeffrey, the youngest, spent most of his time by Mom's side, which rarely included visits to the basement.

The year after we moved in, Mom announced she was in the family way. I was over-the-top excited to finally get that sister I always wanted. We older kids were pretty grossed out that Mom and Dad had made yet another baby, and our *eww* faces showed our disdain. After all, come on, Mom was thirty-eight years old, and kinda old to be doing that sexy stuff. Five months later, we young' uns woke up to a note on the kitchen table saying, "hold the fort," whatever that meant. We ran home from school at lunchtime to see if Mom had delivered the new package. Halfway through the grilled cheese sandwiches that big brother Mike made for us, Dad arrived with a proud grin on his face and announced the arrival of our new baby brother, Darren Robert Howard. I was devastated, ran to my room and like any eight-year-old kid who doesn't get what she wants, screamed, cried, and carried on.

After a few weeks, the cute little gaffer grew on me, and I became the little mother. At just over a year, Darren took his first few wobbly steps in the hallowed space of the basement that we shared with nasty centipedes. It was here that all six Howard children began a lifelong addiction to TV Shows like *Hogan's Heroes, The Beverly Hillbillies, Gilligan's Island, I Dream of Jeannie,* and *Flipper.* We had our eyes glued to the console set almost every day. No doubt this time was a lifesaving hour or two for my mother to enjoy a little serenity before her hooligans started screaming, yelling, and fighting with each other. The big treat of the year was watching *The Wizard of Oz* and eating dinner downstairs on TV trays; we thought we were so special.

The main level of our house was the feeding ground for the six hungry baby birds in the family nest. The lot of us would tuck in around a simulated wood, extend-o-table covered in a clear plastic table cover. We'd recite the "Come Lord Jesus, Be Our Guest" grace and then the feeding frenzy would commence. We ate fast in order to be eligible for seconds, except for Jeffrey, who was usually still eating when the rest of the tribe had been excused from the table.

Fighting over whose turn it was to do the dishes was part of the whole clean-up hullabaloo. My bowels were highly trained to go into action on the nights I was assigned to wash dishes. Worked like a charm for a while until my siblings got wise to my devious ways.

The remainder of the main floor was like a shrine. The living room and dining room were designated a "no-kid" zone except for holidays and special events. As we got a little older Mom would leave my older brother, Mike, in charge when she went out for a few hours and we'd do what any normal kid would do ... sneak in and snoop and lie all over the good furniture.

Our family had the swankiest living room furniture in town. It was framed in solid walnut and covered with nubbly wool bouclé fabric. The super-sized couch had pillows standing like soldiers along its back. There were two "George Jetson-style" lounge chairs to match.

I know for a fact Mom spent weeks shopping for a living room set. She wasn't good with decision-making so finally Dad decided for her. Frustrated, he went out one day to Home Outfitting Furniture Store and bought this big, bright, beautiful, burnt-orange and goldenrod-yellow upholstered furniture. It was anything but pastel.

The dining room set, which had belonged to Dad's parents, did nothing to enhance the modern look we had going on in the living room. It was heavy, dark, ornate, and looked and smelled like the 1800s.

Mom trekked up and down the three flights of stairs—one up, one down, and one in the middle—so many times a day over the years that varicose veins forced her to have three separate operations on her legs. She blamed it on "carrying all you darn kids." I blamed the stairs.

We had one big bathroom upstairs that we all shared; it sported an aqua coloured tub, toilet, and sink. The downstairs powder room was mainly used by the boys. The eight of us had allotted times when our rhythms kicked in and we had it down to a fine art most of the time. Mom, I believe, got used to holding it until the brood left in the mornings for school.

Oldest to Youngest: Michael, Steven, Philip, Lois, Jeffrey, Darren

The upstairs bathroom was the only room lucky enough to have wallpaper—a big, bold, orange, black and gold floral frenzy. Yup, no pastels. Aunt Lillian, Dad's eldest sister, came from London, Ontario to help Mom paste it to the wall. I adored my Aunt Lil as she introduced me to the glam life. She painted my wee toes scarlet red when I was four and I was hooked for life. It took her an hour "to put on her face" in the morning as she was, quite honestly, lily white.

Walking home from school one day back in 1966, I opened the side door to the garage and met my brother, Steve, as he entered the garage from inside the house. He was walking his bike out and tears were streaming down his face.

"What's wrong?" I choked out, my chin shaking.

"Nothing, go inside. They'll tell you." I tore into the house and slammed into a tsunami of sadness; everyone was bawling like when Bambi's mother died in the movie.

Left to Right: Michael, Jeffrey, Lois, Darren, Phil - 2014

I was told my eleven-year-old cousin, Robbie, Mom's younger sister's son, had died. He and his friend had been going door-to-door selling painted glass pieces to collect money for the blind and they had been catching a ride on the back bumper of a milk truck. The milkman didn't see them and accelerated suddenly. Robbie's friend jumped off right away, but my cousin didn't, until it was too late. He went right under the wheel of the vehicle. People had referred to Robbie as "slow" which made him even more precious and lovable to the family. Now he was gone.

The trauma from his early demise was the first death in the family for us children. It took sorrow and loss to a whole new level. My Aunt Donna never fully recovered from her son's passing, and my mother once told me she felt guilty for all the children she had.

It was now the seventies and we older kids took turns washing our hair under the bathtub faucet in the main bathroom with Herbal Essence and Gee Your Hair Smells Terrific—okay, that one was mine. Dad cleaned oil furnaces for a living and he elected to use the laundry tub in the basement to wash up and scrub the oil from his arms, hands, and fingernails with bleach.

I was all hepped up about my upcoming confirmation and Grade 8 graduation. Around this same time, we started getting these bizarre phone calls at weird times, day and night. The caller would hang up as soon as we said, "Hello." Dad started working a lot more nights and we wouldn't see him until morning, which seemed odd. We kids laid low while our parents cold-shouldered it for months as the tension mounted and the atmospheric pressure went down in our house. Dad got the stink eye from Mom every time he walked in the door. We had no idea what was going on, but we felt the strain and knew something was amiss. When Dad was home, he kept busy in the garage, under the hood, or in the basement tinkering with his homemade wine, making himself scarce.

"If Mom and Dad get a divorce, who are you going to live with?" I asked my brother, Phil.

"Dad," of course. That was my plan too. Mom was hard to live with because she was always yelling and screaming at one of us; her fuse was short, so we kept our distance, otherwise the belt would appear out of some obscure hiding place.

My parents were having a huge blow-out one afternoon in the middle of the living room, of all places. Dad was minding his own business reading the newspaper in the roomy gold chair to the right of the fireplace. I had crept in earlier, thinking if Dad could enjoy the peace and quiet of this comely room, so could I, plunking myself in the other lounger and began reading my Trixie Beldon mystery novel.[1]

Mom, with plate and tea towel in hand, frightened us both as she reeled from the kitchen into the living room and confronted Dad about something or other, with spit and fury flying. Tears, anger, and misery made ugly on Mom's face. Dad was not a violent man by nature, but the raised blood vessels in his face and the roar of rage that sprang from deep hidden places within him spoke otherwise. All sense of decorum hightailed it outta there when she threw accusations, ultimatums and, finally, the dinner plate at him. It clocked him right in the face and shattered in three pieces on the floor, leaving a one-inch gash on his right cheek, oozing blood down

---

[1] The Trixie Beldon book series was written between 1948-1985. The first six books were written by Julie Campbell Tatham, and the following 33 titles were written by various in-house writers of Western Publishing under the pseudonym, Kathryn Kenny.

his shirt and onto the gold ottoman.

I have no recollection of where the rest of my siblings were during this brouhaha, nor did anyone ever mention it. Every time I looked at Dad's face from then on, I saw the scar, both on his face, and in my heart.

It turned out that Dad had fallen in love and was having an affair with a woman called Ada at the office where they both worked; she was already married as well, but to an abusive Italian man. Brawls and uproar between the parents and the siblings became common in our home life and reflected the wash of emotions the family was dealing with. Mom told us during a particularly nasty confrontation that this was not our father's first tawdry dalliance. We learned new words and added them to our vocabulary: slut, philanderer, and promiscuous. Ah, the things you wish you could un-hear. This scandal was the hot topic on the lips of friends, family members, neighbours, and parishioners at the Lutheran church for some time, as separation and divorce were not common in our white, middle-class Christian circle. Poor Mom was horrified and ashamed, having to face all these people with the truth.

I was fourteen when Dad left, just after Christmas, 1972. Mom announced to us children that our father was no longer going to be living with us. Before he left, my oldest brother, Mike, happened to be home when Ada's husband knocked on our door and handed my mother a love letter—written by my father—that he'd found in his wife's purse. Mike made it his mission to serve and protect our mom from that moment on and refused to see or talk to my dad after he left to cohabitate with "the other woman." Within a year, all three of my older brothers, aged 21, 19 and 17, scattered like ship rats for higher ground, leaving me, Mom, Jeff, and Darren at home to tend the battle. Ada, though we were not allowed to mention her name out loud anywhere near Mom, was twenty years younger than our dad, who was forty-two. "Ada-Patada," as we called her, would formally become our stepmother within two years.

She and Dad lived together for the first few years in an apartment, awaiting the finalization of our parents' divorce. After that they bought a modest bungalow which suited them perfectly.

Mom hadn't worked outside the home since she had been in her teens, so she was forced to take night classes to update her secretarial skills. "We're going to have to tighten our belts around here," she warned us.

After seeing to my chores, I'd hide in my room or take off on my bike to my friends' houses. Val and Kelly were safe spots to land from "Dr. Jekyll and Mrs. Hyde." Being around Mom was like poking a hornet's nest. Mom retreated into herself with wine and self-help books. I heard her say to her friends over the phone that her nerves were shot, so we three kids tried to be good and helpful. We were treading on eggshell territory, where the lashing of the tongue was worse than the strap.

Sadness and anger left their mark on me the day Dad left. I would have done anything to go live with him and Ada, but guilt gnawed at my innards for betraying Mom just thinking of it. I was left behind, despite being Daddy's little girl. My esteemed station at the top of the totem pole was lowered considerably.

The first thing to go after Dad got his walking papers was the hideous colour on the front doors of our house. A man from our church was offered the job of covering the orange-eyesore with a pleasant pastel green.

Discussions on child support, alimony, and legal matters became the new normal.

The two younger boys, Jeff and Darren, did their visitation run every other weekend. Darren, the youngest at age six years, complained that Dad worked while he was visiting. Ada was the one who babysat and entertained the two kids with cartoons, colouring books, card games, and food. Lots of food. Ada was Italian and an unbelievable cook.

I didn't see much of my father. I saw him when he picked the boys up or when he showed up to grab something he'd left behind from the garage at our house. He invited me over to their two-bedroom apartment a few times and I went, but it was weird. My dad had turned into this hip, boozin', smokin' swinger, so I'd decided on a separation of my own. My father's happiness was in bloom and the rest of the family's spirit was in the toilet. Frankly, I didn't see him busting his hump to spend quality time with any of his kids, so

I decided, "fuck this shit."

I was well into my fifteenth year now and busy with high school, a part-time job at York Theatre, and the task of getting dinner on the table by the time Mom got home at six o'clock in the evening. She'd secured a nine-to-five job at Hiram-Walker's, the liquor people.

One day my second youngest brother, Jeff, passed me an envelope with my name scrawled on the front in Dad's distinctive handwriting. It was a letter. I felt barfy and had to sit down. I opened the envelope and skimmed the letter looking for words I wished to see ... miss you, love you, forgive me, I want you here with me. I got three of those four. I reread the letter three times. "Life is too short not to pursue every ounce of happiness, dear daughter" is the line I will take to my grave.

The next time I saw my father was at the wedding of my eldest brother, Mike, to which Dad wasn't invited. This was like a knife to my heart when I learned he wasn't invited to the ceremony. I was one of five bridesmaids, whose turn it was to step-touch, arm-in-arm with my usher down the aisle towards the church alter. Two steps in, I saw my dad out of the corner of my eye sitting alone in the last pew of the church.

I slammed the lid on my anguish and forged ahead, eyes on the groom at the front of the church. I prayed my brother, Mike, wouldn't see Dad before his bride was by his side so he could focus on his vows and not on vengeance.

The wedding celebration, just over a year after Dad left, was a painful reminder of Mom's sorrow and humiliation as the jilted wife; it was like picking at a barely healed scab. She was happy for my brother and his wife, Bernice, but nonetheless, she grieved as she sat alone in the front pew of the church with her two young boys.

I was in Grade 11 when my brother, Phil, called the house from his new digs saying, "Hey, what are you doing today?"

"Going to school, you idiot. I'm just about to leave."

"Dad's getting married today at 1:00 p.m. Wanna go?"

"Oh, I guess, um, okay. Good excuse to get out of class."

"I'll pick you up from school at noon, okay? Meet me at the auto shop doors."

"Just us?" I asked.

"Yep."

We sat among the well-wishers, some of whom we recognized. The simple ceremony at Barton Stone United Church in Hamilton went by in a blink, and we were invited back to Dad and Ada's cramped, two-bedroom apartment for the reception. They were both over the moon that we came. Raucous jokes, back-slapping and kissy-kiss face ensued while the cocktails were distributed and consumed lustily. The smoker-and-drinkers' tongues got thicker and the music got louder as the afternoon wore on.

Dad bowed at the waist, offered his hand, and asked me to join him in a father/daughter dance on the living room rug. All the glassy-eyed guests stood around us and witnessed this tender moment with oohs and aahs. I felt like I was in the arms of a stranger who now pounded back the liquor, which was never his style. I was no longer that little girl dancing in the kitchen with her wee feet on top of his.

My father kissed me when the song ended, and it landed half-way between cheek and mouth. I pulled away, shocked. I looked up into his boozy eyes and they pleaded for forgiveness.

"Thanks for coming, Yo Yo. You have no idea how much this means. Love you, honey." Liquid sadness seeped down his cheeks and he swiped it away.

Phil and I left the party early—having downed a few rye-and-gingers—reeking of cigarettes and perfume. My brother dropped me off at the house. Jeff and Darren would be home from school shortly, and I had to wash up, change my clothes and get dinner started. Mom never knew we'd watched the re-tying of the knot that had just been untied a short time earlier.

Dad's new marriage was the catalyst for bringing my one-sided separation agreement with my father to an end. We carried on where we'd left off; this new home atmosphere was much more open, free, and happy, because, of course, he was. My anger and pain got filed away under "suppressed" to be dealt with years later after his passing. Prior to that, the fear of losing my dad's love and affection was just too great to risk digging too deeply.

I got myself a boyfriend, finished high school, did a year of college, and moved out of the house just after I turned nineteen. Ahh, freedom at last! I hooked up with three other gals, all nurses, and we rented a townhouse together. I had been offered my first full time job in sales and marketing at the Allan Candy Company and I accepted with pleasure. Because we got loads of free samples of chocolate Easter bunnies, licorice, Swedish Berries and much more, I was super popular with all my friends and family members. Another sweet bonus was meeting Pat P., who worked in accounting, and would one day become my Maid of Honour.

Seven years after the divorce, Mom married husband number two, Roger, and he moved into the ol' homestead. The landscaping got a facelift and the inside of the house got a fresh coat of paint — in pastels, of course. Roger had six kids as well, but they were all grown up and on their own.

Dad and Ada never had children together, and for that I am grateful. She'd had four miscarriages with her first husband. Ada confided in me after being with my dad for a number of years that she wished she had been able to give my father another daughter. It felt like a punch to the gut. Inside my head, I screamed, "There's no fucking way I'd ever share my dad with anyone." I think, by the look on my face, she probably realized it would be wise to not bring this subject up again in my presence. From that day on, my relationship with Ada had a subtle but permanent stain on it.

I grew to love my stepmother, though, with each passing year. She was kind, loving, and generous with each of us kids and kept the family together through birthdays, holidays, and other celebrations. We had a few clashes over the years, she and I, the first one over the idea of her having a kid with my dad. Another was when she wanted to go back to the Catholic Church to receive the sacrament of Holy Communion. The sticky glitch was that she had to adhere to the church's rules on divorce: if she wanted back in the fold, my parents' marriage would have to be annulled. Well, this totally sucked, and I told her so. When I told my siblings they were pretty bent out of shape, too. Ada, coming from a strict, religious, Italian background, had been a devout Catholic all her life, until she hooked up with my dad. After ten years with my father, she made her way back to her parish attending Mass not one day, but seven days a week. Even though she was never granted the right to receive the Eucharist, she dedicated her heart, soul, time, and money to the church, which gave her both spoken and unspoken rewards in the years to come.

Finally, peace reigned in the land again. Mom was happy and it reflected in and around her. Roger and Mom were married for twenty-two years until he died of complications due to diabetes. Dad and Ada made it to their twenty-fourth anniversary. Dad's second wife was forty-seven when she passed away from pancreatic cancer. My father was devastated at losing his best friend.

Mom and Dad reconciled over the years. My wedding was the impetus that united them after nine years of being apart. It was unsettling and uncomfortable, but it set a precedent in the coming years for many more family celebrations and life events to follow.

My parents lived into their eighties. Dad had dementia and forgot he and Mom were not together and would often hold her hand during family gatherings. Phil even caught them kissing in a hallway. We both reacted with that "yuck" face when he told me what he'd witnessed.

William Edwin Howard, our dad, went to the big fishing hole in the sky first. Shirley Irene Penhale Howard Collins, our mother, met her Lord and Maker a year later, leaving their six children, Michael Richard, Steven Roy, Philip Edwin, Lois Donna Shirlene, Jeffrey William, and Darren Robert with years of heartfelt memories and loads of laughs. Us kids all say how grateful we are for the wicked sense of humour and playfulness we inherited from our dad, and for the great care Mom took in teaching us manners, honesty, generosity, and kindness, all supported by her strict moral Christian compass.

Missy Behaving

My cousin, Lori, and I were born nine days apart, which made her more like a sister than a cousin. She lived in London, Ontario, just one and a half hours away from me in Hamilton.

From the age of six, every year we took turns staying at each other's house over the summer holidays, and we'd plan our sleepover week before the school year ended. In 1965, it was my turn to host, and we decided to start our little holiday on June 27th.

My aunt and uncle pulled up into our driveway that day in their blue station wagon with the fancy-schmancy wood side-panelling. The car was stuffed to the rafters with their five kids, a cooler jam-packed full of food, books to amuse the youngest children during the long drive, and one single suitcase. They would head back down the highway—one kid short—at the end of a fun but exhausting day.

The first house my family lived in, with me in it, was at 299 West 2nd Street. It was the same shape as the red ones in the Monopoly game but with white siding and a yellow front door. The houses on our street were small but the yards were ample. The front stoop was big enough for me and a friend from the neighbourhood to play with our Barbies. There was a side entrance too, its door also yellow, and it had a metal screen door with diamond shapes in it. I know this because I froze my tongue to it one winter. Boy, that was dumb; won't do that again. Right beside the side door was the milk-man's hidey-hole where he dropped off the milk bottles. We also had a back door entrance off the kitchen that also sported a screen door, but it was wooden, and it made a mighty slam when the wind took it.

It was 1965 and The Rolling Stones were all the rage, *The Sound of Music* was the movie to see, and "Sorry about that, Chief" was a phrase made popular by TV spy Maxwell Smart on a show called,

Get Smart. Lori and I were only seven years old at the time and we were playing in the yard and chasing after Buttons, our cat—who was jet black with little white booties—when I heard my mom calling me. I carried on trying to catch the cat.

"Lois Donna Shirlene Howard, you answer me this instant. I know you heard me," she shouted.

Well, that stopped me in my tracks. Trouble was amiss when she blurted my whole darn name out loud. I hoped and prayed none of the neighbours had heard.

Kissin' Cousins: Lori, Lois, Cathy

"What?" I bellowed back, rolling my eyes at Lori.

"Come here please. Don't make me yell. When I call you, I expect you to answer, Missy." I always got the "Missy" when she was miffed at me.

I lollygagged my way towards her as she stood with her left arm holding the back screen door open.

"What am I going to do with you?" she tsked, tsked. I didn't have an answer for that, as my eyes locked onto the green prickly curlers with the pink sticks skewered through them. They marched row-by-row up one side of her head and down the other. She typically kept her curlers covered with a colourful kerchief. She'd even sleep with those pokey things sticking into her head. Suffering this torture usually meant she had a church meeting or a friend coming over for coffee. If her hair wasn't dry in time, her back-up was to put what looked like a shower cap attached to a portable dryer on over the curlers. Mom would sometimes grumble that many of the ladies on the street got their hair done once a week at the beauty parlour and "it might be nice if I could too," but having six kids to feed wouldn't allow for such a luxury. She often referred to herself as "the old woman in the shoe" as a reference to a nursery rhyme which has had different versions since the 1700's, but nevertheless has been told from generation to generation.

"Lo-ee, we're out of milk and the milkman doesn't come until tomorrow. Run over to Johnny's store and get me a pint of homogenized milk. Mimi's coming over for coffee a little later.

"Can Lori come too?" I asked.

"No, Lois, it won't take you long. Leave her to play with Buttons. Go on now, quick, quick." She stuffed a paper bill in my hand. "Go straight there and back and bring back the change ... all of it." She let the door slam behind her as Jeffrey, my little brother at the time, was screaming up a storm, as usual. I walked over to Lori, told her what I'd been asked to do, told her to stay put, then bee-lined it as fast as my short legs would go.

Johnny's was down-the-street-and-turn-right close. It was a little neighbourhood variety store attached to a house, where the owners lived. It was candy dreamland for little kids. You pointed out to the store owner what you wanted behind the glass case and they'd pack up anything your heart desired—Pixie Sticks, Double Bubble, Mo-Jos, blackballs, marshmallow strawberries, gumdrops, Black Cat gum, mint leaves, Lik-M-Aid or licorice cigars—and pack it all into pint-sized, brown paper bags. You name it, they had it. Except for the Popeye cigarettes, licorice cigars, and Lik-M-Aid, candy was three for a penny.

I ran home in a flash with the milk in tow and waved to my cousin who was twisting round and round on the swing, coiling as tight as she could so the "uncurl" would be sensational.

There was no sign of the cat.

Once I got her attention, I yelled, "Be right back." She nodded in return.

I opened the back door to our place, called out I was home, and put the milk and money on the floor inside the door. I ran back to the swing set where Lori was waiting.

"Wanna see what I got you?" Her blonde ringlets bobbed up and down. "Close your eyes, put out your hand, and you'll get a big surprise."

Lori held out her hand and I plunked a big fat, juicy marshmallow strawberry in it. Her eyes lit up and she promptly plopped it in her mouth, creating a little pouch in her cheek. "These are my favewit," she sighed with delight. I smeared the residual red goo from my hands onto my pink pedal pushers feeling quite pleased with myself. Lori worked away on the sugary lump, swallowed, then asked, "How did you get this? Didn't your mom say to bwing back the change?" I guess my cousin heard us talking.

I shrugged and dug deep in the pockets of my "drawers," retrieving some of the loot. I planted one of the sweet red chewy delights straight into my mouth, savoured it for a sec, then gobbled it down in two seconds flat in case Mom was watching from inside the house; she told us kids she had eyes in the back of her head.

"What if she finds out, Lo?"

I knew Mom didn't really count the change. How do I know? Well, just the previous week she had sent me on another run to the store for her Cameo Menthol cigarettes. She asked for the change back then as well. Before I got home, I unloaded a whole box of Cracker Jacks down my gullet; I even had the hidden prize from inside the box to prove it: a green plastic whistle. I dumped the empty box down the sewer on my way home.

All in all, this errand business was becoming very lucrative. I shared this last escapade with my cousin, and her face went all shocked. She was such a goody-goody. I grabbed her by the arm and dragged her to the teeter-totter, which was a part of our swing set. I sat on the seat that was resting on the ground, bent my legs, and pushed up high enough to hover half-way so Lori could easily mount on her end. We began a slow teeter, then I ramped up the speed by putting more thrust in my legs for more totter. We upped and downed it with varying degrees of velocity until I got bored and chose to implement the "jump ship" tactic. With my end of the teeter-totter's seat slamming to a halt on the grass, I scrambled off, causing Lori's end to crash to the ground, making her teeth rattle. I laughed at the look on her face even though I hated it when my stupid brothers did it to me. My cousin started to wail, her mouth wide open with the red guck from the candy oozing from her crybaby face.

Mom came tearing out the back door with Jeffrey on her hip, yelling at me, "What did you do?"

When she saw Lori's face, her face faded to white and her hand flew to her throat. "My word," she exclaimed. "Did you fall off, honey?" Mom rubbed Lori's back saying, "You're all right, sweetheart, you're all right," in a soothing voice. "Let Aunt Shirley see where you're hurt."

Mom jumped up and ordered me to stay with Lori and my brother while she ran to get a cold, wet washcloth.

"Mom," I said. "Mom!" I cried out, while she walked further away.

Turning around, she said, "What?" with an exasperated tone.

"She's not really hurt."

"What are you talking about? You can see there's blood."

Here goes, I thought to myself, *I'm doomed.*

Sucky-face, Lori blubbered, "She made me fall off the teeder-

23

tawdder, Aunt Shirley." Mom glared at me with daggers then asked Lori if she'd bit her tongue when she fell.

Her curls did a side-to-side dance this time. "Uh, uh, it's stwawbewwy.

"What?" Mom asked, looking confused.

Pointing at me, Lori ratted me out saying, "She stole money from you. You told her to bwing back all the change, but she didn't. She bought candy and gave me some. See? She opened her big fat mouth and showed off the remnants of the evidence.

Mom's eyes went all hard and squinty when she looked at me and asked if this was true.

I nodded, head bowed.

"I've told you never to lie, Missy. Get in the house this instant." She gave me a sound whack on the bum and finger pointed, "to your room. And say you're sorry to your cousin."

"Sorry, Lori." I said, meaning it.

I was relieved she didn't say Lori would have to go home before our holiday week together was up, even though my cousin had finked on me. I didn't put up a fuss about going to my room either; I could now savour the last of the sweet, buried treasure in my pocket in peace.

The many cherished summer weeks of escape to my cousin's house during my formative years were never boring, to be sure, and were instrumental in shaping the me I am today.

The next summer I turned eight years old and visited Lori and her sister, Cathy, who was two years older than us. The first night of my visit, they decided to enlighten me about the visitor who came to me after I fell asleep at night.

"Who's that?" I asked.

"The Sandman," they answered nonchalantly.

"What's a Sandman?" I asked.

"When you're asleep, he puts sand in your eyes. But you can't see him, 'cause he's invisible," Cathy explained in a spooky, whispery voice.

I gulped and said, "I don't believe you."

"Ya know that crusty gunk in the corner of your eyes when you wake up in the morning? The Sandman puts it there!"

I fought long and hard to stay awake lying next to them that night, but I guess I surrendered to sleep because the next morning I awoke with the dreaded eye crud. It took me months to get over the image of this bogeyman entering my room until my brother, Phil told me it was just a stupid prank made up to scare me.

When I was nine years old, I was plagued with yet another new level of terror, beyond that of those stupid flying monkeys in the *Wizard of Oz,* compliments of my cousins, once again.

Cathy, Lori, and I slept in the same bed in the middle bedroom at their house. The room was painted forget-me-not blue. The bed faced the outside window which looked out into the backyard. Close to the house was a ginormous oak tree that looked as old as Rip Van Winkle—the old guy who fell asleep for twenty years in the story of the same name. During violent thunderstorms that summer, the wind whipped its leaves and branches into a tizzy, which sent me into a tailspin of fear, terrified we'd be hit by lightning.

Lying there, Cathy whispered to me, "Do you see that?"

"What?" I asked, straining to see whatever it was I was supposed to see out the window.

She told me a story about a witch who lived in the old tree.

"She's mean and nasty and hunts little children and steals their thoughts," Cathy said.

"I'm not that little," I reminded myself. Nevertheless, I laid there with my eyes glued open all night. Sleep was elusive for the duration of the visit. Blankets up to my chin, I kept looking out, haunted by the idea of my thoughts being stolen.

Two days before the end of my visit, Aunt Phyllis asked me how I was feeling. She grabbed my chin and moved it to-and-fro, looking deep into my eyes. Lips quivering, I whimpered, then let out a resounding sob, "I wanna go home!" I spilled the beans on the witch saga, Cathy got a good talking to for tormenting me, and I got closure that neither me nor my thoughts would be snatched away at the hands of a wicked witch.

As I got older, a permanent decision was made between the families that my summer holidays would be spent in London, not at my house in Hamilton, and the visits were extended from one week to two. I was thrilled and relieved because life in London was calmer and quieter away from my five brothers and my mother. Not only that, but my Aunt Phyllis, the third oldest of Dad's sisters, was a lot more easy-going and waaay cooler than my mom. The other plus was she worked during the day which gave us kids plenty of non-supervised time. My Uncle Lorne worked long shifts as an engineer with CP Rail, and when he was home during the day, he slept. At night, when we three girls were hunkered down in bed, he would toot the engine's horn sending us a "goodnight", as the train chuff-chuffed along the tracks behind their house on Cayley Drive. Cathy and Lori's two older brothers, Ron and Tom, who were artists, had moved out at a very young age, which left one brother, David, or "Crockett," as we called him, home with his two younger sisters. He came and went as he pleased, which, all added up to more free, FREE, FREEDOM for us girls.

I put my mother through Hell when I hit the tween years. My legs were beastly back in Grade 6. Two boys in my class called me "gorilla legs." I was mortified as Mom forced me to wear ankle socks even though I bemoaned the fact that I had legs like a man. Ankle socks were for babies. She caught me red-handed in the garage putting on knee socks, which landed me another smack on the ass. So, I did what any other eleven-year-old kid would do—I discreetly stuffed the knee socks in my pocket and changed into them at school. I shared my woes with my cousin, Lori, over the phone one evening when Mom was out and she told me not to worry, that she and her sister would hatch a plan on my next visit. I had no idea what that meant, but I knew they'd think of something.

Mom drove me to London this time. Usually, either Mom or Dad would put me on the bus from downtown Hamilton, with a pack of Butter Rum Lifesavers for company, and Aunt Phyllis would be there on the other end to pick me up. Once Mom and I arrived, we hugged and kissed hello to my aunt and cousins, sat and had tea, then Lori whispered in my ear, "go to the bathroom," so I took the hint and did. While I took my time doing my business, my two cousins confided to my mom the hairy leg dilemma and how the boys were making fun of me.

"Aunt Shirley, our mom lets us shave our legs, you know. It's no big deal," Cathy stated.

"She's only eleven! I don't want her growing up before her time." I'd heard this time and time again in the past few years.

"Shirl, what harm can it do? You don't want her to be teased and laughed at do you?" Aunt Phyllis asked with wide eyes.

I was elated to have this team as my back-up because my mom soon caved. My aunt suggested the adults go shopping for a few hours and when they returned, Mom handed me a large shopping bag. "For you." Peeking in I spied the holiest of holies ... a razor, just like the one Dad used. And not only that, in this same bag was also a chocolate brown corduroy pantsuit with a cool zipper up the centre of the tunic adorned with a large metal pull-ring. I couldn't believe Mom did this for me. I was overcome with love, gratitude, and a dollop of guilt for being a part of this devious set-up to get what I wanted. But wowee, a razor and a mod new outfit; my grin was amped at full wattage.

Mom drove home to Hamilton that evening leaving me in the company of these relatives I loved and adored. The next day, it took two razors, (my cousins used theirs too), four blades and two determined girls to dehairitize my legs ... top, bottom, back, front, sides and even my toes. Oh, how I loved my new shiny, smooth, naked look. A weight was taken off me, and not just from my legs.

To cap off the best summer ever, two days following the shearing of my pegs, cousin Cathy suggested they pierce my ears. "Oh, hell, ya!" I shouted. I'd begged Mom the last few years to get my ears pierced, but she always responded with, "Why do you want to grow up so fast?"

With a steady hand, Cathy marked the spots on my ears with a pen where the needle would go in, so they'd be even-steven. She had an extra set of gold "keepers" she was gifting to me. There were four of us enrolled in this epic adventure – Cathy, Lori, Cathy's best friend, Joy, and me. We raided the fridge for ice cubes and used them to freeze the first ear. In case you were wondering, my aunt and uncle were both at work and expected to be home around dinner time. Cathy poked the sterilized needle (cleaned with rubbing alcohol) into my right ear, got half-way, turned green, ran to the bathroom, and threw up. Sitting there with the needle looking like an arrow on a bullseye, the rest of us laughed our guts out at the predicament we were in.

"Who's gonna finish the job?" I shrieked.

Joy looked stupefied and shook her head, "No way."

I gotta say I was sorely disappointed as Joy was a pretty cool chick and had a mouth on her that would make our Pastor blush, but she shied away, looking ready to bolt. My eyes begged Lori. She was up for the job, and she pushed the needle clean on through, the needle making *"pop pop pop"* sounds as it penetrated each layer of skin. My brave new hero tackled the next earlobe, inserted the "keepers" and I was open for business, though soaked in sweat and feeling shaky. Lori looked a little wobbly too. I doused the puncture wounds with alcohol for three months straight as I was instructed by Cathy and never had an issue with infection.

Mom picked me up from the bus station days later and noticed my ears when we sat down for dinner that evening. She hit the roof ranting and raving about the bad influence Lori and Cathy had on me, as well as giving a long boring lecture on, you guessed it, "growing up before my time." My brothers sat there in silence, which was highly unusual, attempting to catch a glimpse of my new piercings. Dad was working, so he missed all the drama. I sat there listening to Mom's wrath but refused to let it interfere with the happy glow I was feeling from these precious rites of pubescent passage that I'd never, ever forget.

Spending time with my aunt and uncle and their kids was my ticket to tranquility for the next few years as there was a whole lotta' shit going down at my house in the early seventies. Mom and Dad were dancing around the D-word—divorce—and the seas were angry, my friend.

With each visit to my cousins', I subsequently earned the merit badges of teenage-hood. Lori and Cathy were way ahead of me in maturity and exposure to "grown-up" things and I was their willing minion. Make-up, boys, bras, and tampons were next on the roster of initiation. Mom was opposed to them all, most assuredly the tampons as I was informed only mature women were allowed to wear them.

"But, why?" I asked.

"Because I said so."

I took it upon myself in Grade 8 to investigate the mystery of those tampon things. I was in a gymnastics competition the following day, and there was no way I'd be caught dead wearing a sanitary belt and a giant mattress between my legs. So, I tootled off to the drugstore, got home, opened the package, and inserted the Junior-sized tampon, as had been suggested to me at the store. After one cartwheel it popped out; I was aghast and cut the day short. My friend, Val, gave me a brief tutorial on the correct way of putting it up and in and I never looked back. Mom was none the wiser until she found a box of "Super-sizers" in my drawer many months later. She just looked at me with sad eyes, shook her head which said, "You know how I feel about this."

Every time I arrived home from London, I was a more informed initiate, which added to the greying strands in my mother's hair. I wished my mom was more like my Aunt Phyllis. I loved the relationship my cousins had with their mother. They were able to talk to her about important things and my aunt encouraged them to do so.

At sixteen, we gals all had part-time jobs during the school year and full-time jobs during the summer which changed the dynamics of the visits somewhat. Boyfriends with cars entered the scene upping the ante for more teenage tomfoolery. Yes indeedy, at this tender age I graduated and received my "Grew Up Before Her Time" certificate thanks to my dear, devoted cousins and their mother who always had my back, my legs, my ears, and most importantly, my heart.

The Furnace Man

I wrote this letter to my father, William Edwin Howard, in the 1990s. It was found in his belongings when he passed away in 2014 and my brother, Mike, read it at his funeral.

M y dad's hands worked hard, and they smelled bad. I envied my friends for their fathers' glamorous vocations ... professor, draftsman, contractor, postman. My dad cleaned furnaces.

In fourth grade our teacher, Miss Westbrook, asked us to share what our fathers did for a living in a detailed written report due the following day. After supper that night, I approached my dad and told him about the homework assignment. "Isn't there a fancier name for what you do so I don't have to tell the class you're a furnace man?"

He laughed and patted the seat beside him on the couch. I crawled up beside this man I adored and cuddled up tight. He said, "You can tell them I'm a Heating Technician." My heart burst with pride and my face went from worried to wonder-full. My Dad, the Heating Technician. I rehearsed the line in my head then headed to my room to begin my story.

Today, the smell of furnace or engine oil syncs with my olfactory organs reminding me of my Daddy-o. I would climb into his dirty, stinky red truck with the company name, "Standard Fuel Oil" painted on the sides in golden yellow. The vehicle carted gizmos, gadgets, vacuums, tools, pipes, and pails of asbestos, all dedicated to the upkeep and maintenance of people's oil furnaces.

At all hours of the day or night, Dad's job required him to be "on call." The dispatcher at head office would contact him by phone with a customer's name and address, then off he'd go in his big truck. Occasionally, he'd invite me to go along with him. We'd gab and giggle, and he'd share his roll of Crysto Mint Lifesavers, which sat on the middle console along with spare change and pencil nubs. Dad was forever singing or whistling, an endearing habit I also picked up. He'd click on the radio, and we'd hum along in unison. I'd stare at his beefy hands as they asserted their strength and control on the steering wheel, then look at my own hands to see if they looked the same; our thumbs kinda looked similar, which made me proud. His stained fingers with the black stuff underneath the nails would tap out the beat of the music on the dashboard. The only time his fingernails were really clean was before he went to bed and on Sunday mornings for church. It took bleach and a knife's blade to scrape the oil from beneath the nails. I'd wait for him in the truck as he doctored the heating hurts of the greater Hamilton area.

My father knew the first and sometimes second line of every song, I swear, then hummed along to the rest of the lyrics. One of his faves was, "It's a Long Way to Tipperary" but his version was, "It's A Long Way To Tickle Mary," which cracked the family up. "I Left My Heart in San Francisco," "Sentimental Journey," and "Linda" were on the top of his chart favourites too. This timeless first-line trait has been passed down to all six of his kids and we always laugh when we are reminded of where it came from. We then recall all the corny songs he'd sing, and we sing them, too.

Thanks, Dad, for the little things that remind us of you, which, really, in the end, are the ones we remember the most.

I love you,
Your daughter,

Lois

31

Tell Me a Story

This is the story of an old 78 record and three storybooks which influenced my childhood.

One of the most precious possessions we owned as kids was an old 78 rpm record (78s became standard in 1910, in case you were interested). It was entitled, "Tell Me A Story" and it was sung by Frankie Laine and Jimmy Boyd. It was a goofy song that burrowed a space somewhere in the young noggins of my brothers and me, and still remains a beloved life-long tenant.

My Aunt Donna, Mom's sister, passed along many of the records, books, games, and toys that had belonged to her son, Robbie. Our sweet cousin lost his life when he was eleven years old having been run over by a milk truck. It was a tragedy that none of us Howard kids ever forgot. I was seven years old at the time, and it was the first funeral I ever attended ... and totally freaked me out.

The song is sung by an older dude but it sounds like some dufus kid. I always imagined the freckly, red-headed kid from Mad Magazine singing the lyrics. It goes:

> *Tell me a story,*
> *Tell me a story,*
> *Tell me a story, remember what you said.*
> *You promised me you said you would,*
> *You gotta give in so I'll be good.*
> *Tell me a story then I'll go to bed.*

The song is about a little boy pestering his father to read him a bed-time story after the dad is just home from a long day at work. "Tell Me A Story" was born in 1953 and in keeping with the times, you hear the kid getting his hide tanned, "whack, whack, whack," because he's tried his father's patience. It's disturbing to hear this form of punishment today, but me and my four brothers loved this part of the song the best because we could so relate. Spanking, slapping, hitting, and washing your kid's mouth out with soap were accepted forms of keeping them in line at this time in our history. Life lesson here, Little Lo ... if you piss your parents off, there are consequences. I will *never* forget the taste of Dial soap as long as I live—for saying the f-word, of course.

Our cousin, Robbie played this record repeatedly when we would visit his house, before he went off to Heaven, which is why the song has such an emotional connection to me and my brothers. Every so often this goofy song will pop into the heads of one of us six Howard kids and it takes us back to sillier, simpler times, and to our cousin, Robbie, as well. It keeps his spirit alive in all of us.

Being read to as a child was akin to Dad driving us kids, clad in our jammies, to the Stoney Creek Dairy for an ice cream cone on a Saturday night in the summertime. I believe it led me into the de-licious world of words, books, stories, and learning. I don't recall Mom reading us bedtime stories when we were young, back in the fifties and sixties, but I could be wrong. No doubt, by the end of the day, she was "shaked and baked" and needed her downtime. Occa-sionally, though, Mom would break into song with "You Are My Sunshine," as well as a sweet little ditty her father had made up about the two dogs she grew up with on the farm in St. Thomas, Ontario during the forties. It went,

Tippy and Toby were two little dogs,
They went together on two floating logs.
The logs rolled over and they tumbled in,
And Tippy and Toby got wet to the skin.

I do remember my Grandma Penhale (Mom's mom) reading to me while I stayed with her when my littler brother, Jeffrey, was born. I was four-years-old. All the kids except Mike, the oldest, were billeted out to other family members, and Grandma got me. I don't remember the name of the storybook, but with the patience of Job, she'd repeat the story at my every urging.

I'd curl up with her on the scratchy, green-pea-coloured arm-chair which sat beside the fireplace in the living room. The text it-self is blurry in my mind, but the little picture book comes to my dreams to this very day. It contained images of horses, black and white cows, green pastures, red barns, and pink little pigs. This farmland visual is like a pacifier for my mind. Grandma and Grandpa used to live on a farm, or so I was told, and this little kid's book brought me to a place where I could imagine a real-life farm. They were now city folk.

The gem I gleaned from this wee story was the glory of reading as a gift, both for oneself and for others. My heart was full and happy in that prickly green chair that cradled just me and Grandma. I had her all to myself and those memories live on.

I eventually learned to read myself, and when I entered my early teens, Trixie Belden made a surprise appearance. This Trixie Belden book was a gift from who-the-hell-knows now. What I do know is this spunky young tomboy-ish girl was my "Shero" at the time. She was old news by the time I got my hands on one of her books as publication of her thirty-six adventures began in 1948.

Once introduced to the young heroine of the series, I begged for more books to fill me up, nourish, and inspire me. Trixie's a thir-teen-year-old, super-sleuth who gets the job done. She's not afraid to go eye-to-eye with the bad guys. She was a leader in an age where "fitting in" was expected, especially for young girls. Not my Trix though ... she dressed, thought, and acted with courage and confi-dence, even when she got into precarious "sitiations." Her best friend, Honey, was the poor little rich kid who was afraid of every-thing and tended to be a sickly child – a perfect contrast to her friend, Trixie. I vacillated between Honey and Trixie's personalities back then, and still do.

You know that question, "What Would Jesus Do?" in times of strife? I replace it with "What Would Trixie Do?" That's how much her moxie informed my life back in the late sixties.

A nother favourite book of mine was *Chicken Little*, also given to us from our Aunt Donna, mom's sister, as part of her son's far-too-short-a-life collection. Being eight years older than my youngest brother, it was my job to read to him before he went off to la-la land each night. I surmise the before-bed reading ritual began once we had these story books in our possession. We five other kids all grumbled to Mom that the youngest was getting preferential treatment and we got ripped off!

In the story, an acorn boinks Chicken Little on the top of his head from a tree above, which leads him to believe the sky is falling. He convinces his friends, Henny Penny, Goosey Loosey, Ducky Lucky, and Turkey Lurky of this grievous notion. They all agree to follow Chicken Little to see the King to report the calamity.

On the way to the castle, they meet the dastardly Foxy Loxy, who tries to lure them into his lair, assuring them they'll all be safe. He offers to go to the King himself to report that the sky was falling. But Chicken Little gets wise to his trickery when he remembers the sage advice that someone had once told him that "birds are supposed to stay clear of the fox."

Chicken Little and all his barnyard pals scurry home to safety and agree to be careful in the future. Believing the world was coming to an end all because a tiny acorn plopped down from the heavens was a little far-fetched, they all admitted in the end.

This simple folktale was written in 1840 by Hugo Silver. Upon investigation of the original story, (thanks, Google), Chicken Little's innocent, naive pals actually were lured into the fox's den and, one at a time, were ripped to shreds and beheaded. Their bodies were thrown one way, their heads the other.

Come on, really?

The fox's last victim, of course, was poor Chicken Little. "Foxy Loxy caught hold of the little guy and ate him all up, then finished his supper with the rest of the gang, and all of this from the foolish fright of Chicken Little."

I am forever grateful I never read the original text to my little brother. He'd have been scarred for life.

What I did learn from this simple narrative is that just because you think something is true doesn't always make it so.

The last of my favourite books from girlhood is *Harriet the Spy*, which is why I saved it for last. This book was published in 1964 and written by Louise Fitzhugh.

I was sitting in Miss Harris's Grade 6 class. She wasn't my most-liked teacher at Buchanan Park Public School, not by a long shot. I soured against her because she gave all her praise and attention to the "browners" in the class and ignored the rest of us.

One day I complimented her on a pretty dress she was wearing and she came back with a sneery response that said something close to "stop sucking up." There were other students standing around her and I was hurt and mortified. I will give kudos where kudos are due to this teacher, however, because of the Friday afternoon story time ritual. It was the highlight of my week. Miss Harris instructed us to place our heads down on folded arms on top of our desks and just listen as she read. No complaints from me. None at all. It was a glorious treat to just listen and not have to make notes.

Harriet the Spy, AKA Harriet M. Welsch, is an eleven-year-old girl in the fifth grade whose dream it is to become a writer and a spy. She is the only child of well-to-do parents who live in New York City. Her curiosity and head-strong personality—qualities of paramount importance in becoming a spy—lead to peeking, snooping, and prying into the lives of her neighbours, friends, family members, and classmates.

Harriet has kept a notebook ever since she could write and goes nowhere without it. Her journal records all the private thoughts, observations, and opinions she has about everyone on her spy route.

The family's live-in nanny, Ole Golly, is a very important and stable fixture in this young girl's life. She guides Harriet with authority, wisdom, and fondness.

Harriet's life falls to ruin when she loses her coveted notebook and her two best friends, Sport and Janie, find it, read it, then share it with the rest of the class. Her classmates are furious at the cruel and mean comments she writes about them and vow to get revenge. They all refuse to talk to her. To make matters worse, Ole Golly announces that she has received a proposal of marriage, and she leaves the Welsch family home for good.

Hostility and resentment continue to grow between Harriet and her classmates; they get back by pulling hurtful pranks on Harriet. Harriet is full of rage and despair from losing both her friends and her nanny. The torment and loneliness are unleashed on anyone in her path, where previously it was reserved only for her journal's ears. The principal of the school confiscates her notebook during school hours, so Harriet refuses to attend school but soon finds herself bored to tears with her own company.

Ole Golly, now living out of town, sends a letter to Harriet advising her to write an apology to her friends and classmates, and to get back to the work of becoming a serious writer.

Harmony is restored when Harriet writes and submits an apology for publication in the school newspaper. She then returns to school and the principal subsequently offers her the position of Editor on the newspaper's staff.

Harriet the Spy was banned by schools and parents alike not long after it was first published. After all, it did not support the belief that "children should be seen and not heard." The spirited young heroine displayed independence, unruly behaviour, and apparel unsuitable for a young lady during the sixties. In addition, her lying, cussing, spying, and speaking her mind was thought to set a bad example for other children.

May I say a big THANK YOU to Miss Harris, the cranky,

crunchy, unfair teacher that she was, for not drinking the Conformity Kool-Aid. I am grateful to her for exposing me to this wonderful example of how much courage and determination it takes to "be yourself." This can mean letting go of living up to other people's expectations and demands, as well as the perpetual people-pleasing we all know so well.

As I write these words, I am aware of how much Harriet and I had in common. We loved writing, hated math, began a love affair with our journals at an early age, studied humanity, and were devoted, heart and soul, to our friends.

This classic story for young people grants all of us, young and old, permission to be ourselves.

"Tell Me A Story" song was written by Terry Gilkyson and performed by Jimmy Boyd and Frankie Laine, Released February 13, 1953 by Columbia Label

The Remarkable Story of Chicken Little was originally written and published in the City of Boston, Massachusetts in 1840 by John Green Chandler. Katharine Pyle then published her 1918 version in *Mother's Nursery Tales*. In 1958, it was re-written by Marjorie Hartwell and published Western Publishing. Today's version is based on the earlier two examples of the story, and published by Harper Collins, June 17, 1987.

Harriet The Spy was written by Louise Fitzhugh, published by Harper and Rowe in 1964, United States.

Mrs. B.

I trudged the two blocks to 32 Columbia Drive every school morning at approximately 8:00 a.m., Monday to Friday, except for holidays and sick days. I rapped my signature knockity-knock-knock on the front door just like I'd been doing since Grade 3.

Mrs. B. opened the door and waved me in with her warm, sunny smile, even at this early hour. My mom could be cranky in the morning, so this was a lovely reprieve from the usual. She sported her customary early morning attire: pink hand-knit slippers, nightgown, and coral-coloured chenille housecoat. There was never a hair out of place; it looked the same morning, noon, and night on account of it being "pixie" style, just like Mia Farrow's. Its light brown shade with the frosted tips would serve her well in her "senior" years, always making her look younger than her actual age.

"She ready?" I'd ask.

Her impish blue-green eyes would scoff at my silly query. We all knew mornings were not her middle daughter's finest hours.

"Tea's on." Mrs. B. said. This was my invite to the family breakfast table. Tea was always on in this house, it was an Irish ritual ... Mrs. B.'s ancestry. Milk in the cup first, then add the steaming dark liquid, she instructed me the very first time I joined the family for this early morning gathering. The heavily steeped, stand-a-spoon-up-in-it black tea was poured from a colossal brown teapot that had its own little hand-crocheted cozy sweater to keep the contents warm.

Once the hot liquid comfort was served, the kids, the ones all dressed and ready for school, pounced on the huge stack of butter-soaked toast made from real Wonder Bread. We all smothered Kraft peanut butter and homemade strawberry jam all over our breakfast toast, then dove in for seconds.

39

I didn't mind waiting for Kelly, not one bit. I had felt kindred to the Berkopec family ever since I had struck up a friendship with Tina, their eldest daughter. She'd been my buddy since Grade 3, but after a few years my mom said, "That girl is growing up before her time." I was discouraged from hanging out with Tina, which was just as well because she developed very early and became a "woman" at a very young age. This left the rest of flat-chested, sexually uninformed innocents behind in her wake. The boys sniffed the air and smelled the pheromones and swarmed like honeybees. Tina became boy crazy and part of the "cool" gang in Grade 6, which left me out of the fray.

Along came Kelly, the next sister down. You know that saying about doors closing and windows opening? She was a brainer and had skipped a grade. In the fall of our Centennial year, 1967, she happened to be in my class, and I just picked up with her where I had left off with her older sister.

Mrs. B. was my life-rope. She brought consistency and peace to my otherwise chaotic home life. I had five loud, rambunctious brothers and a volatile mother. Dad's work cleaning and fixing oil furnaces had him doing calls at all hours of the day and night. My parent's marriage was like Italian bottled salad dressing ... clear oil on top, and the mysterious dregs on the bottom. Dad was the working rooster and Mom the stay-at-home mother hen. The temperature between the walls of our house went from hot to cold, and not by way of the thermostat, for many years.

I spent lots of my spare time holed up in the Berkopec's basement, especially during and after Mom and Dad's divorce when I turned fourteen. Kelly and I would lament to the sorrow of the song, "Tell Laura I Love Her." We'd shout the lyrics, "look out, look out, look out," when Tommy's car overturns in flames in the song, and when they pull him from the twisted wreck, his last dying words are, "Tell Laura I love her. Tell Laura not to cry. My love for her will never die." The two of us would topple heartbroken onto the basement floor in typical tween-age tears. "I'm Henry the VIII, I am" by Herman's Hermits is another song we'd belt out line by line over and over repeatedly. We'd gab for hours on end about school, boys, sex, sewing, and makeup. That lower sanctum in her home, and her family's acceptance and understanding of what I was going through, was like Noxzema on a sunburn.

Mr. Berkopec would come through the door after work and often see me sitting there in front of the boob tube with his kids— Tina, Kelly, Holly, and Joe Jr.— and say, "Are you here again?" I didn't take offence 'cause he always had a twinkle in his eye when he said it. He liked to tease me, which I enjoyed. He'd say hello to his offspring, then call out, "Sam, I'm home." I never knew why he addressed his wife by this name and didn't have the nerve to ask. His wife's real name was Muriel. After kissing his "Sam" hello as she was preparing dinner in the kitchen, he'd wander back into the living room, shoo us kids out, sprawl on the floor in front of the television set, light up a smoke, and turn the dial to the news. I guess his mom never told him it wasn't good for his eyes to sit close to the TV set. His wife would place a bowl of mixed nuts or potato chips and a beer in front of him on the floor. This was his quiet, "Dad-time" until supper was announced. It was obvious he loved to eat because he looked like Mr. French, the portly butler on *Family Affair,* the popular show back in the late sixties that we watched religiously. We couldn't get enough of Buffy, Jodie, or Cissy. Their uncle Bill, played by Brian Keith, was raising his newly orphaned nieces and nephew with very little experience in raising children. Lots of silly antics ensued.

What I loved and admired most about Kelly's mom was the friendship she shared with her three girls. Chat sessions took place around the kitchen table after school and on weekends while guzzling copious amounts of tea and eating homemade cookies. After the age of sixteen we ladies were allowed to join Mrs. B. for a smoke. My mom would have had a fit had she known. Before heading for the home front, I'd wash up with soap, water, and a facecloth, then spritz with Charlie perfume to remove the stench. Mrs. B. was a part-time smoker and preferred menthol cigarettes. She was very "with it," when it came down to the toil and troubles of female adolescents—hot guys, monthly cramps, zits, and "what am I gonna be when I grow up?" kinda stuff.

Mrs. B. planned a visit to see her parents one day. Her mom and dad lived on the East side of Hamilton, and she invited me along with the whole family. I felt honoured and excited to meet the couple who had raised her. These two little white-haired leprechauns kept us entertained for the duration of our stay. Mrs. B.'s father was no bigger than my twelve-year-old brother. He sat in a well-worn recliner surrounded by clouds of smoke. There was never a time he wasn't puff-puffing on an unfiltered hand-rolled ciggy with his nicotine-stained fingers and moustache. Room was at a minimum in their house, their furniture taking up most of it. The elder Mrs. ran around getting seats for everyone. It appeared Kelly's Grandma was a knitter, as both she and her husband sported bright green and yellow socks on their feet.

"I really like your slippers," I said, which made everyone smile. I'd noticed that each of Kelly's family members wore the same comfy footwear around the house but each had a vibrant colour all their own.

I'd never heard an Irish accent before, other than when the little green guy on the Lucky Charm Cereal commercials would say, "They're magically delicious." I was enchanted with Mrs. B's parent's Irish banter.

It was time for tea, and out came the massive teapot which was covered in a green knit tea cozy sweater, as well. Grandma passed around a plate of peanut butter and chocolate chip cookies. I'd concluded this was how the traditions had been passed down. Grandpa, however, opted for his whiskey, which he tossed down in one swig in order to get back to his smoke. His ashtray was begging to be emptied.

Kelly and I worked at the York Theatre in Hamilton a few evenings a week and on Saturdays when we were thirteen and fourteen. She was the concession gal and I sold the tickets. We had a blast, but I ate more than I earned. I gained not only experience in dealing with people and handling money, but also ten pounds and a face full of pimples from all the chips, popcorn, and candy I plowed through.

In high school, Kelly was a cheerleader and had to attend

numerous basketball, football, and every other "ball" games you could think of. I'd attend when I wasn't working at my new office job at Home Outfitting Furniture in downtown Hamilton. My brothers, Phil and Steve, got me in as they worked in the shipping department. I was sixteen at the time. Cheerleaders weren't allowed to work as their practice time was heavy and unpredictable.

Kelly and I, decked out in our bell-bottom jeans, peasant blouses, and platform shoes, were yapping away as we walked the halls of Westmount High one day, books in hand, when a good-looking, dark-haired guy walked by us. "Hey, Kelly," he smiled and then looked me in the eyes and nodded.

"Isn't he on the basketball team?" I asked, once he had passed by.

"Yup. Football as well. Nice guy." Kelly replied.

"What's his name?"

"John Lenarduzzi. His brother, Henry is running for school president."

"He's cute. That's some last name, huh? Must be Italian."

Days later John Lenarduzzi asked Kelly about me. "Who's your friend with the piano-teeth smile?"

I thought that was a very bizarre thing to say, but at least he had noticed my smile.

I screwed up the courage to ask John Lenarduzzi out on a date to the Sadie Hawkins high school dance months later and he accepted. From then on, we became inseparable.

Busy with boyfriends, part-time jobs and homework, my friendship with Kelly lost speed. We still got together but didn't have the time to play like we had as kids. She dated a man named Dave who was much older than her. I tagged along with them one day doing who knows what, and I was acting my usual goofy self—Kelly and I had our own corny baby-talk banter. Kelly turned around, looked at me, and said, "Lois you are so immature. Why don't you grow up?" I was hurt and embarrassed, but realized our relationship was changing ... we were growing up.

After high school, Kelly pursued a career in banking. We remained relatively close for the next four years. Some years later, she married a really nice guy named, Barry, and they settled in Edmonton. They had a child later in life after trying for many years, much to the family's delight. To be closer to family, they eventually moved back to the Hamilton area, which is a blessing for Kelly's Mom, Mrs. B.

And that high school sweetheart I was dating? I ended up marrying that handsome son-of-a-gun on August 23, 1980, after going out together for five years. I was twenty-two and he was a year older. I chose Kelly to be one of my six bridesmaids. We had a big, traditional Italian wedding planned, capped off at two hundred and seventy-five guests. Good Lord, it was crazy. Frankly, I was overwhelmed by all the wedding preparations, packing up my apartment in Hamilton, quitting my current job at Allan Candy, and finding a new one in Toronto. The thought of moving to a new place in the town of Pickering where I knew absolutely no one, save John, was leading to sleepless nights and anxious days. To add some spicy pepper to the soup, my poor mother was driving me koo-koo as she anticipated the upcoming wedding with jitters usually reserved for the bride or groom. Nope. She didn't want to have any part of this event if my father was going to be there. "But Dad's walking me down the aisle, for crying out loud. I only have one father!" I said firmly. She relented on this fact. Then I broke it to her that dad's wife, Ada, would be his guest at the wedding. Well, that broke the sound barrier. No way, no how, was my mother coming to the wedding if "she" was there. This shindig would be the first formal event my mom and dad would be together socially for after their not-so-amicable divorce, almost nine years earlier, and consequently my mother fussed, mussed, and meddled in every detail. I was ready to cancel the whole G-D wedding. Thankfully, time does soften things; by the time a year of wedding-prep-mania flew by, Mother had loosened her grip on things and conceded to be there for me, which allowed a deep, resounding breath of relief to be released by yours truly.

Before our nuptials, my guy had secured a job at Ontario Hydro after a two-year training period up in Deep River, about 200 km north-west of Ottawa. A week after we got married, I began working at Maclean's Magazine as the office manager in the Advertising

Sales Department. We went to the Poconos, PA, for our honeymoon for that blessed week, during which I slept and cried for most of it, feeling so depleted physically and emotionally from all the hoo-hah. I absolutely adored working in the publishing world, but the com-muting back and forth to Toronto got to be "a pain where a pill won't reach"—one of Grandma Penhale's quirky sayings—after eight years.

We bought our first house in Pickering a year after we were married, as we decided apartment living was a bit too cramped. We did a fair amount of entertaining with occasional sleepovers—both John and I come from families of eight and that whole extended lot of siblings, their partners, and children, not to mention our high school friends and the "Hydroids" (friends we met at Ontario Hy-dro). From Pickering, we decided to move to Whitby and had a house built. However, after seven years, the traffic got to be stupid and we started looking elsewhere. I had quit my job in Toronto and joined the Metroland newspaper world both in Oshawa, then Markham. I then landed a job selling advertising for Homes Maga-zine in York Region.

I was driving home one day and decided to take a different route by way of Coronation Road, just north of Whitby, in the quaint town of Brooklin. I drove by a small hamlet of homes and turned left onto Philip Street (one of my brother's names). Every house in "Macedonian Village" (as the posted sign called it) was different and unique. This was not currently the trend in the building industry during the early nineties; they were building cookie-cutter houses that all looked like little boxes. I took a right and drove down Shepherd Road, where, lo and behold, there were two lots for sale. My heart exploded with excitement to share the news with my honey, so I took a quick drive around the village, and discovered the other street out to the main road was called Steven Road, (another one of my brother's names). Well, this was just God messing with me and I wanted to play too, so I raced home to tell John.

We bought one of those gorgeous 100' x 225' wooded lots, and planned to build what would be our second custom-built home. When building began, I decided to go back to school to become a massage therapist. I was thirty-seven-years-old. After getting my certification, I and another registered massage therapist (RMT) opened Brock Therapeutics in downtown Whitby, close to the 401, to begin our practice. We stayed in the Brooklin home for more than twenty-five years but decided to downsize closer to where we were born and raised—Hamilton. Now living in Ancaster, I was now closer to old friends from high school and family and could connect with those I hadn't seen for some time, like Mrs. B., as well as Mom's dear friend, Helen. These ladies hold an anti-lock, secure, never-to-be-tampered-with soft spot in my heart for life.

Mrs. Muriel Berkopec's love for me was rock solid ... I never doubted it. She oozed kindness and never said a cross word to me in all the years I knew her, in a home where I always felt safe. She smelled of warm biscuits and Ivory soap and I loved her with all my heart.

She is now a widow no longer living in the family home on Columbia Drive, some fifty years later. She and Kelly even surprised the hell out of me when they showed up at my mother's funeral on September 22, 2015.

Special people can show up in our lives to help us along the often, unpredictable road. I believe Mrs. B. was a fairy godmother to me for a good part of my first two decades of life. I am forever grateful for her unfaltering love and support.

You Take a Piece of Me with You

Ricky Bryans was my first. I didn't get all moony about him until Grade 4. His every word and deed took up way too much space in my head than my mom would ever have approved of, if she'd known. He was planted in my life the first day of kindergarten and we shared our school years all the way up to Grade 12.

Ricky had an impish grin, soft brown eyes and dirty-blond curls that topped the tips of his ears at a time when brush cuts were the trend. Whenever he'd say something to me, I'd panic, my hands feeling like wet washcloths, my heart thrumming like a tom-tom drum. So, I'd ignore him by turning away. Of course, I'd race to get a seat near him whenever I could, if and when the opportunity arose.

Ricky was best buds with Anthony, the brainiest kid not only in our class, but in the entire school. The two of them sat at the front of the room so our teacher, Miss Nicholson, could easily call on her star pupil, as well as keep her eye on the problem child, Ricky.

My dream boat lived just up the street from me. In the early years, I'd peddle by his place on my bike in the evenings or weekends hoping to catch a glimpse of him. I don't recall ever admitting my infatuation with this boy to any of my friends other than Kelly, who was my best friend. It was my guilty-pleasure secret.

I was eight years old when my brother, Phil, accused me of being a virgin. This insult was flung at me while our legs pumped with great force competing for who could swing the highest on our swing set in the backyard. I denied this accusation with a vengeance, but he just wouldn't let up, and continued to taunt me. Furious, I hurled myself off the swing with an impressive arc and ran into the house yelling for Mom. She appeared, tea towel in hand, asking what all

47

the commotion was about. "Mom, Phil keeps calling me a virgin, and he won't stop," I cried. Mom tore down the back steps and hauled mister smart aleck into the house by one ear and proceeded to give him a good spanking. "That'll show him I'm no virgin." I said to myself smugly.

When I was nine this same brother told me babies were made by men putting their "things" into a girl's privates. I was mortified, and it was "totally not true," I assured myself. Pain-in-the-arse that he was, Phillip was my informant around the forbidden ... meaning, sex. He squirrelled away dirty magazines in the crawl space fort he'd built beneath our house. Posted on the outside walls of his lair were hand-printed "No Trespassing" signs. On the inside walls were pictures of naked ladies with bare boobies and bushy hair "down there." When the coast was clear, I'd sneak into Phil's den of iniquity and steal some of his stash of candy and quick peeks at the nudies. With my sex education well in hand, I was now equipped with the knowledge and know-how to pursue the "other" sex.

Funny thing is, once I started giving Ricky certain "looks," he was totally oblivious to my subtle attempts at flirting. Mom was right, girls were more mature than boys at that age.

It was 1969, the year of Woodstock, "Get Back" by the Beatles, and the Manson Murders. My mom ran into Ricky's Mother, Janine, at Loblaws. "Come on over Friday afternoon for a gab, Shirley," Mrs. Bryans said, "and bring the kids. They can go for a swim." Ricky's family was the first on the street to have a swimming pool. *Hot-diggity*, I thought when Mom told us about the invitation. I had visions of my guy and me frolicking like Frankie and Annette—*Beach Blanket Bingo*-style—but in the pool.

It was a scorcher that Friday. We arrived, got settled and I politely asked to use the washroom in the house; I really just wanted to see inside the Bryans' house. Their washroom was roomy and spotless with fluffy white hand towels hanging on the towel rack. My family of eight were not guest-towel worthy; my brothers were slobs. As I cruised through the kitchen towards the door to the backyard, I sniffed the remnants of toast, coffee, and bacon. I

walked back into the brilliant sunshine to where the moms sat yap-
ping in loungers on the patio beside the pool, sipping bottled Coca
Colas and poofing on their cigarettes. Mrs. Bryans set out cherry
Kool-Aid and peanut butter cookies for us kids.

Ricky and my two younger brothers, Jeff and Darren, cannon-
balled into the deep end of the large rectangular pool and started
wrestling, which meant game over for me. I waded in the shallow
end in my robin's egg blue, two-piece bathing suit trying to hide my
sulky face. I dipped in and out a few times, but only to my shoulders
because I didn't want to get my hair wet. The three animals bellowed and tumbled in a tangle of boyhood trying to dunk one another. As they moved closer to me, I removed myself from the
splashes and tomfoolery to sit in a lawn chair by the ladies, but
Mom gave me a look that thought otherwise, so I sat over in the
grass on my towel.

A whole mess of biological weirdness was taking place in my
body then with much to follow. Humps, bumps, and hair where
there shouldn't be. The only thing that didn't change radically was
my crush on Ricky. He started to talk to me more, maybe because
another boy in our class asked me to be his girlfriend and word had
gotten out.

When our Grade 6 graduation finally dawned—I got to wear
pantyhose for the very first time, after months of begging Mom to
let me—the ceremony and dance were held in the school gymnasium.
I lost all feeling in my legs when Ricky walked over and asked me to
dance. I paused for "station identification"—you weren't supposed
to look desperate—then said "Okay." We slow-danced the first one,
"twisted" the second one, then he was gone in a wisp to scout out a
new dance partner. I took it as a good sign that he asked me first.
The girls sat on one side of the gym and boys on the other. He asked
one girl after another to dance, simply by jutting his chin in their
direction, and up they'd jump. They were under his spell; I mean he
was no Paul Newman by any stretch. This bravado prompted the
other boys to follow his lead and head to the opposite bleachers.

Just before the celebration ended, Ricky sauntered over and
asked if I wanted to meet him in the "field," meaning the apple

orchard, the following day. "What for?" I asked, my hands doing that wet washcloth thing again.

"Just to hang out."

"Can I bring Kelly?" I asked. I wasn't brave enough to go by myself; I'd never been in this situation before.

"Sure, I'll get Anthony to come too."

Backing onto our subdivision, separated by a five-foot wire fence, was a massive piece of property with a large hoity-toity private school on it. Butting up against the school property was an old apple orchard with the gnarliest trees you've ever laid eyes on. This is where the kids on my street escaped from nosey-parker neighbours and parents to climb trees, smoke cigarettes, and fool around. "What happens in the orchard, stays in the orchard," was street law.

The "hole-in-the-fence" gang met the next afternoon. We crawled through the gap in the fence someone had thoughtfully pried open, and bee-lined it to the ride situated on the periphery of the private school, about twenty yards from the orchard. It sat all by itself, with no other playground-ride friends to keep it company. No one had a name for this thing; we all called it something different. It was like a merry-go-round but without the horses. We'd run round and round in circles on the perimeter of the ride, hanging onto the bars until we hit top speed then hop up on the platform and spin like the blazes, just before hitting the puking point. When the ride slowed down, we'd hop off, lie down on our backs on the grass until the world stopped whirling and wobble-walk like Dean Martin on a bender to do it all over again.

When the four of us had had enough of self-induced vertigo, we took off like lightning bugs toward the apple trees. We plunked ourselves under an old granddad tree, its trunk thick, dry, grey, and covered in deeply embedded lines. It scratched my back through the pink T-shirt I was wearing when I leaned back against it. I opened the small purple pouch affixed around my neck and pulled out two of my dad's Players cigarettes I had pilfered from inside his truck. He kept them hidden from Mom—she didn't know he'd gone back to smoking cigarettes occasionally but he'd admitted it to me. The matches I scooped from the cupboard that stored the birthday candles. I presented the contraband to my merry band of twelve-year-olds and my eyes asked, "who's in?" All in, it took three match strikes to get the damn things lit.

It was the first lame attempt to inhale for Kelly, Anthony, and me, resulting in coughs, sputters, and gags.

I stood up from the hard ground and almost keeled over. My head felt woozy and my face turned a weird colour, or so Kelly told me. I walked away slowly, taking deep breaths to get my balance and pride back. I didn't want to make a fool of myself in front of my friends, especially Ricky, but he followed me anyway.

"Hey, wait up," he cried out. He touched my arm and asked if I was all right.

"Yup," I lied.

"Can I kiss you?" he asked.

I glanced over at Kelly who was busy watching Anthony climb a tree, attempting to score an apple for her. That boy really was one sweet guy. The two of them were too close for what Ricky had in mind, and I didn't want anyone to witness our private business, so I suggested we walk in another direction, which was kind of a "yes" to his question. We sat on the orchard floor blanketed by scrubby grass and weeds, and that's when he made his move. His right hand cupped my right shoulder and his lips came in for a landing on mine. I was shaking as his lips pressed hard and insistent. He tasted like cigarette, which further nauseated me, and I turned away. He grabbed my chin and advanced again, pushing my lips open with his. Then his hand started making its way up my shirt. I slapped his hand away, which I guess he interpreted as, "she wants more," and tried again. Holy cow! I jumped up and brushed the shame and debris off my shorts.

"Kelly," I yelled to my friend. I ran toward the sound of her voice answering back. I looked back at the disgust on Ricky's face. My eyes gushed, with a sob hell-bent on coming up and out. I stopped mid-way, bent over with hands on my knees trying to slow down the pounding and breaking of my heart. My heart told my head this wasn't his first time kissing a girl.

I arrived early at school that Monday morning, sat down and opened my desktop to retrieve my writing supplies. Unfocused eyes ran over the questions assigned to us over the weekend, which I hadn't completed, which was not like me. I decided then and there that boys can mess your life up.

Kelly walked into the classroom and I greeted her with a sad smile; she volleyed one back. Before taking her seat two down from me, her hand settled on mine which ceased the nervous pencil thumping on the desk I hadn't even been aware of.

"Are you okay?" she asked.

"Asshole," was all I could come up with, referring to "you know who."

Ricky finally showed up to class with his posse in tow. He threw a fake-punch toward Ronnie Savin's face as he passed by his desk; Ricky turned his head around with a snicker and a sneer making sure "his boys" caught his bravado.

Ricky never even looked my way that entire day, which both inflamed and consoled me.

I am now in my sixth decade and I've seen my old flame from time to time over the years. I never regret making like a bandit versus "making out" like a bandit because I was in way over my young head and it scared me. Good thing, too. Good ol' Rick is now on wife number three which proves to me that my heart and my head had, and will always have, my back.

Past, Tense

Directly below the portrait of Queen Elizabeth II to whom the class sings, "God Save The Queen" and pledges allegiance, stands Miss Kane with her back to us. She drones on about the history of The Hudson's Bay Company while making notes in point form on the chalkboard in her perfect loopdiloo handwriting.

A kerfuffle ensues diverting the focus of the student's attention from the early explorers to the commotion in the back of the room.

Johnny Lea horks up a sizeable phlegm-gem. He holds the unrivalled record at Buchanan Park School for champion spit-baller. It's all about tongue placement, taking good aim, and blowing through the hollowed-out pen casement. It impresses the guys and grosses out the girls. Nobody, but *nobody*, wants to be on the receiving end of one of those babies. Johnny's popularity as the "bad boy" hinges on picking on the weak and defying anyone with authority.

Johnny lines up his shot and fires. The gooey ammo whizzes straight for the back of Ronnie Savin's razor-shorn noggin'. Bullseye! Ronnie jumps up and around in his seat to confront the dirty dog who flicked the offensive slime bomb. Giggles and guffaws hide behind covered mouths as the kids witness Johnny's latest victim suffer this cruel humiliation, relieved it wasn't them.

Miss Kane senses unrest in her classroom and whirls around to face those who have the audacity to interrupt her lesson. She scans the room, lips pursed, eyes narrowed and sharp, hands on her hips. Each student, save two, sit up ramrod straight, arms on their desks, hands folded. This long-time teacher was born with the senses of a bloodhound and the disposition of a Doberman.

"Would anyone care to share what's so funny?" she screeches. Silence. "Anyone?" She bores into their terrified faces with the oh-so-familiar stink-eye.

Johnny glances around the room with an arrogance far beyond his years, daring his peers to rat on him. Most of the children's eye-balls work the room like pin balls, claiming wide-eyed innocence, all except for Ronnie Savin's. His eyes pull away from, then magnetically lock back onto the teacher's.

"Young man, stand up this instant," she bellowed.

Poor Ronnie stands up with a tremulous smile, wiping the glob from the back of his head onto his rusty-brown corduroy pants.

"What do you have to say for yourself?"

"Nothing," Ronnie's hands clench and unclench, his tongue pokes out to moisten his white, crusted lips.

Some of Johnny's goons laugh and taunt him, while others mime the twirl of an index finger around the ear.

The attention spurs Ronnie on and he laughs with everyone else in the class.

"Mr. Savin, if you think this is so amusing, perhaps you would like to entertain the principal in his office, hmm?"

The perpetrator, Johnny Lea, folds his arms and crosses his legs like a grown-up man with a smug look on his face. He makes eye contact with Mary Gillis, the teacher's pet, challenging her to report him.

Mary sticks her tongue out at the insufferable bully, only after checking it was safe from Miss Kane's line of vision. Johnny blows her a kiss followed by a wink.

The teacher bulldozes her way towards Ronnie's desk and clamps her claw-like fingers onto his stick-like arm. He tries to pull away from her grasp. His books, papers, and pencils tumble from desk to floor while the other hand waves frantically in the air for help. Ronnie grunts and squeals then hurls himself back into the safety of his seat, eyes registering fear and confusion. Miss Kane is on him like cops on a criminal and hauls his skinny frame up from the chair and parades him across the front of the classroom towards the door.

"I will be back shortly, boys and girls. While I am gone you will write in your workbooks, "I will not laugh in class again" one hundred times." Before her and her rat's-nest beehive leave the room, she shouts over her shoulder, "Rest assured, I will be check-ing your work."

She yanks Ronnie out the classroom door and down the hall to the place every kid fears: Mr. Cooper's office. This guy made Miss Kane look like that nanny who served sugar with medicine. Our teacher's tirade to the principal concerning her expectations regarding student decorum is heard echoing the hallways. Back in the classroom, Johnny lets out a long, slow whistle then sings, "Ding-dong the witch is dead."

Some kids laugh, but guilt and remorse hover in the heads of others. Most are uneasy about losing Johnny's favour, though. Oth-ers are too busy writing their lines while envisioning the big, black strap lying on Mr. Cooper's desk. Mary, sitting in the front row, turns her head and barks at the troublemaker sitting in the back row, "Johnny Lea, that was a very mean thing to do to Ronnie. You might think it's funny, but it's not."

The students grow quiet, everyone taking a collective breath in, waiting.

"Like I care," he throws back at Miss Goody Two Shoes. "He's a retard, for crying out loud. He doesn't understand anything anyway. What's your problem, Mary? You like him or something?"

Mary turns to face the front of the room in disgust and resumes the, "I will not laugh in class again" assignment.

Twenty minutes later, little Ronnie is escorted back to class, his red swollen eyes exuding defeat and bewilderment, streaks of spent tears leaving tiny paths down his ravaged face. His hands were red and raw. The teacher points her finger towards his desk and com-mands him to "sit" with her eyes.

Miss Kane's cheeks are the same colour as Ronnie's hands. With her hand resting just below her throat, she instructs the students to stop writing and face her. "We shall commence with our Social Studies lesson. Please turn to Page 382 in your readers."

"Oh, but Miss," Mary pipes up, right hand waving frantically. "Are you going to check our writing assignment?"

"Miss Gillis, are you having trouble hearing? Did I not just ask you to open your Social Studies textbook?"

"Yes, Miss Kane."

Ronnie sits at his desk and looks from face to face with a shy, embarrassed smile, snot dripping down onto the top of his quivering lips.

Katie Tyrrell leans over into the aisle when the teacher's back is turned and places a Double Bubble into Ronnie's hand. She gives him a quick smile, puts her finger to her lips with a "shhhh" and whispers, "for later, not now," then turns her attention back to Miss Crab Apple Kane, trying to concentrate on the olden days of explorers like Champlain and Cartier, the Indians, and fur trading in the new world.

Based on a true story on how some of the faculty members in 1968 at my public school treated children with "mental retardation" as it was known back then, now referred to as intellectual disabilities.

Slip Slidin' Away

There's a way to slip away from the drain of the mundane that I discovered at age ten.

Dad surprised me one day with an old clunker hand-me-down he scooped from a customer's basement. He went into lots of people's homes because he fixed and installed oil furnaces for a living. My dad was like the grey-haired guy on Sanford and Son, but without the grey hair. He came home with everybody's old crap all the time. He wasn't quite at "hoarder" status, but was heading in that direction.

I tried to look happy and excited, but quite frankly this two-wheeled contraption was Ug-a-Ly—its newness way, way past the expiry date. No basket, no streamers, no pizzazz. I didn't know how to break it to him that he could return the old wreck. Dad promised me he'd put a new "coat" on her and she'd be "good as new," and I could pick the colour. Together we headed to Canadian Tire, and I pointed to the popsicle purple shade of the spray-on paint. This is how my new/old loyal sidekick got the name, "Poppy, as in poppy-sicle." She became the Abbott to my Costello. I even affixed a few of my brother's baseball cards with clothespins to the spokes of the wheels for that wonderous flippity-flap-flap sound you got when you pedaled your brains out. This began my sweet love of cycling.

The 1960s boasted carefree playtime for kids, in my neck of the woods, anyway. If your chores and homework were done, you were allowed to leave home base for greener, freer pastures ... friends' yards or basements, the park, hiking trails, orchards, corner stores, Woolco Department store, and the penny-candy store. I frequented these places often thanks to my new mode of transportation and independence.

"Bye, Mom; I'm going," I'd yell, minding not to slam the door behind me before hopping on my one-ride, two-wheeled, purple-people-speeder. Buzzing down my street in a blur heading, no doubt, over to my friend Kelly's house, I entered a world of wonder and freedom, where to this day still continues to thrill and exhila-rate me as I cruise around town on my "b-c-klet." Poppy is long gone, but not forgotten.

J.J.

The new girl was starting that day and it was my job to train her as we would be alternately sharing the 7-3 and 3-11 shifts.

As I waited for her to arrive at the Esso Gas Station where I worked, I heard the familiar "ping ping" of a customer driving up to one of the twelve gas pumps. The driver stopped at the Number 3 pump, and I gave him time to climb out of his vehicle, lift the nozzle, and ram it into the gas tank before I pressed the button to engage the flow of gasoline. Welcome to the control centre, where I wielded my power from a ten-by-ten-foot kiosk. I eyed the dude with the mullet as he gave me the once-over, and a weaselly grin. The name, "Kenny" was stitched onto the pocket of his filthy, wrinkled navy shirt. He crushed a half-smoked cigarette between his Popeye lips as he reached down and adjusted his "nads."

I depressed the loudspeaker button, "S'cuse me, sir. No smoking allowed near the gas pumps."

He flicked the butt towards the kiosk.

"Dickwad," I scowled.

A rap on the glass door jolted me. Hand on chest, I opened the door and waved the newbie in. Quick once over—around my age, nice eyes, quick smile.

"Jennifer, right?" She nods.

"Lois," I pointed to myself.

Kenny-the-creep entered the customer entrance of the kiosk throwing a ten-dollar bill at me through the pay hole, as well as a curled lip and the mouthed word, "bitch." I gave him a twenty-dollar smile back.

With the asshole gone, I got busy showing our new recruit the ropes: press applicable gas pump button, take payment, hand over receipt; repeat. It was a no-brainer, part-time job, ideal for me as it allowed time to study for my college classes during the quiet times.

From day one, Jennifer and I got along like scotch and soda. We yapped that first night back in 1975 for eight hours straight about boyfriends, hopes and dreams, shopping, school, our families, and our favourite television shows.

Jennifer's parents were well past their prime for parenthood. Their youngest child was a happy mistake, her dad told me. Mr. And Mrs. Johnson lived in a tired, unkempt apartment building in downtown Hamilton near McMaster University. They spent their waking hours drinking, smoking, watching TV, and arguing. They were the most uncouth couple I had ever met, which was a delight, since I had grown up in a cookie-cutter, Christian household during my formative years.

Jen's parents came from a vaudevillian background – her dad was an actor and her mom, well, she danced for her supper. Though long both retired, they were still entertainers, with colourful stories and language tossed back and forth like hot potatoes. Hearing about their X-rated pasts was a hoot and a half. Their place was ideal for overnight sleepovers: no curfew, no rules, which was perfect for us wild and crazy teenagers, until it came down to our interest in eating at regular times. This family had no set menu plans, family eating times, or any set order of any kind that I could see. I was accustomed to my Wonder Bread living environment. Meal-times, according to Mr. Johnson were, "any god-damned time I feel like it," which for dinner was any time between seven and ten in the evening, as he did all the cooking. Cheese, crackers, and potato chips were the food staples they kept stocked to soak up their liquid meals. Cigarettes were lit up between forkfuls. Strong black tea that knit little furry sweaters on your teeth was one constant they enjoyed after eating. My new friend and I usually skipped out and grabbed Harvey's hamburgers with fries and a milkshake or sometimes pizza. I was invited once for Sunday dinner which consisted of roast beef and turnip mashed with potatoes. That's it, no frills. We ate in front of the television. Jennifer said this invite was an odd occurrence and she shared, "My dad likes it when you come to visit."

Jennifer's mother had tiny, delicate hands with fingers stained a rich tobacco brown which contrasted nicely with the poppy-red nail polish on the fingernails. She imparted the importance of a lady always taking care of her hands, as she patted the grey and I-Love-Lucy-red tufts of hair on her balding head. This wee scarecrow of a lady struggled day and night with her breathing. Jennifer told me her mom had cancer, but not to bring it up in conversation under any circumstances.

Jennifer's father was a big bruiser of a guy, standing over six feet tall. He was a dapper-dandy dresser and loved bright, shockingly colourful clothes. He also shared the same box of hair colour his wife used. He had the ungainly look of entertainer Red Skelton and the brash personality of comedian Don Rickles.

Of course, my mother disapproved of this new friend of mine. *She's trouble. Her parents give her much too much freedom, if you ask me.* She forbade me from hanging around with Jen outside of work. "Yah, uh huh." Mom could have been a preacher's wife; the worst she could do in the cursing department was "damn." She came from a strict Presbyterian background growing up, and saw only black and white, no greys.

My dad and his wife, Ada, however, welcomed Jennifer with open arms. Since marrying wife number two, my father had become more liberal and open with the booze, smoking, sexuality, and swearing. We loved popping in on them. 6He hadn't been like that at all when he lived with my mom and us kids. He had, however, let the big bad "F" word rip way back when I was around twelve years old. I'd been helping him make peach wine and he had just poured the sweet-smelling, pulverized fruit into a giant crockery pot that had belonged to my Grandma Howard, Dad's mom. It slipped out of his big meaty hands and crashed onto the cement basement floor. The rafters shook with his wrath and I ran for the hills, up the stairs to my bedroom. Luckily, Mom wasn't home.

My boyfriend, John, wasn't too impressed with my new buddy ol' pal either. Bad influence, blah, blah, blah. My guy was training at Ontario Hydro way up north in Deep River, 200 kms north-west of Ottawa, and didn't get home for weeks at a time, which left plenty of single gal-pal time for bars, booze, and boys.

Jennifer Johnson blew into my life like a gale force wind the day she joined the Esso Gas Station team. In the eight blessed months we hung out together, I learned a boatload of wisdom from her. Though we were both now eighteen years old, she was way more advanced, seasoned, and ripe for the world at large. I believe her two older sisters, who I'd never met, had something to do with her maturing beyond her years. I was told in no uncertain terms to keep my legs together or I'd end up in the same predicament as "those two." These were the pearls Mr. Johnson passed along to both me and his youngest child that I will keep in my memory bank forever.

Jennifer's personality was as bright and vivid as her Windex-blue eyes; her moods, however, could be as dark as the wavey, raven-black mane of hair that reached the middle of her back.

Had this dear friend not walked into my life, I'd never have bee-bopped with the Herman's Hermits, or hysterically lost my shit when we were asked to "please leave" by the manager of the restau-rant after having smoked hashish at the end of one of my afternoon-shifts at the gas station. We had walked to the Ding-Ho Chinese Food Restaurant a few doors down the street and ordered a number of specials on the menu, as well as the usual fried rice, chicken balls, and egg rolls. The table was laden, but we barely ate a thing. We were too busy giggling, guffawing, and spewing adolescent stupid-ity until we were escorted out. I don't remember paying, but we went home toting heavy doggy bags.

John and I had broken up just about this time. We'd been fighting off and on over the past year about the amount of time he was spending with his family than with me. He drove home about every seven weeks from Deep River to Hamilton, which wasn't a lot of quality time together. I'd be so excited about him coming I'd plan for days what we'd do, where we'd go, what I'd wear, and take pains in fussing over myself for our date night, but would be left waiting for hours on end for him to show up, and I was pissed. After split-ting up, I was immersed in the theatrics of a broken heart. Of course, I sat by the phone pining away until Jen hauled me up by my "poor-me" bootstraps and threatened to slap me silly. "Never ever, wait for a man; have some pride, will you? Don't be one of those spineless women who are nothing without a man in their life." Jennifer told me I deserved to be treated with respect and have some for myself. She believed friendships were very important, and to never ditch them for anyone with a penis. Hmm, my mother told me the same thing sometime after Dad left us when I was fourteen but left out the male anatomy reference. I've left out most of the bad words Jennifer decorated her poetic wisdom with, so as not to offend my readers. That girl could weave every fucking dirty word known to man into an everyday conversation, and totally own it with no goddamned apology given. I believe her parents and upbringing earned her this sage knowledge and advice that she passed along to me, and that I, to this day, continue to pass along to other innocent, naïve women.

Jennifer began dating a guy and I dated his friend, George. George and I didn't last too long, but a month into their new relationship, Jen and Vince were invited to a wedding and she asked me if she could borrow one of my favourite little black dresses. I was happy to oblige but soon lost the do-goody feeling when I needed and asked for it back weeks later. I called her on numerous occasions at Vince's place, with no response back. We had both quit our jobs at Esso, so getting hold of her there was not an option. She stayed at Vince's more often than not, but I had no idea where he lived. As a last resort, I left an angry, bitchy message on her parent's home phone, which I was not proud of. She returned my call saying, "Fine, I'll drop the dress off at your house." I wasn't home when she came, but she left my beautiful black dress filthy and wrapped in a ball, reeking of cigarettes, in a plastic bag with my mother. Boy, did that curdle my colon.

Sad to say, a man came between Jennifer and me, and we never saw each other again. Vince came into her life, and I was ushered out. I mourned the loss of this beautiful friendship-affair, though I am grateful for all she gave me. I just wish she had heeded her own Ann Lander's advice-columnist counsel.

A Biker's Reflections

I gotta admit, I look like quite the serious Mountain Bike Mama in her all-togethers: black biking skort, chartreuse green spandex tank with built-in bra, and matching Nikes. My laces are double-knotted and tucked inside low-ride purple anklets, so I have no fear of getting them caught in the spokes. I plop my Barney-purple bike helmet atop my unbrushed hair, lock and load the chin straps and then slide on my smokin' cool, rainbow-lens sunglasses.

I unzip the 8"x 6" black pouch that is Velcro-attached to the handlebars and take inventory: Kleenex, cell phone, water bottle, and a twenty-dollar bill for "just in casies." After pulling on my riding gloves, I mount my hybrid Giant and make my way to the end of the driveway, craning my neck this way and that, checking for cars and other movables. The street I live on has a dead end, so no rush hour bedlam, but safety comes first.

Pulling onto Shepherd Road, I start with slow, arduous revolutions as the bike is still in low gear from when I'd last taken her out. My pumping maneuvers stretch then shorten my jiggly, lazy thighs, which are whining in protest already. I ease into a lighter gear to stifle the complaints, then pedal my ass out of the little hamlet of "Macedonian Village," where I live with my honey in Brooklin, Ontario. I'm headed toward farm country which lies north of us.

Next, I steer onto Coronation Road and ride for one and a half kilometres until I spy the first of many hills. "Here we go. Oh God." My brain reacts before I even get to the damn thing. Hills don't get me all warm and tingly, but they're a means to an end. I stand up on the bike and give it the old heave-ho acceleration it needs, pushing my legs with all I've got. I make it to the crest of the hill, sit my arse back down on the hard, narrow crotch-killer seat, and careen all the way down the hill, legs and feet stretched out in a "V," howling with a triumphant "woo-hoo."

Within the helmet my head pulses with dah-dumps from the strain and I can feel sweat dampen various creases in my body. My breathing starts to normalize as I work up to a decent clip along the flat, winding road before me. My eyes are on active watch for potholes, rocks, loose gravel, roadkill, and unleashed dogs. The nose and ears are there for support if the "Danger Will Robinson" signal bleeps.

I remind myself to stop looking ahead and return to enjoying what's presenting before me: the birds twitter and twill, the bevy of sweet late summer scents tickle my nostrils, and the squirrels chase each other in a game of tag.

I veer off the familiar onto an unknown dirt path that has beckoned me the last few weeks. It leads into a thicket complete with an enchanted forest canopy for me to glide through and under. There are tight bends and twists ahead that make my shoulders tense up from hanging onto the handlebars too tightly; control is trying to out-wrestle me. I loosen the vice-grip and the turns become smoother, less rigid and jerky, and I feel more in sync with the bike. I lay off the hand brakes, which makes the ride even more steady-eddy as I skirt the puddles and hammer over the stumps, roots, and rocks—the perfect obstacle course for a cyclist. *What an ideal metaphor for life*, I think to myself. The more I slam on the brakes and/or hang on too tight trying to control what shows up in my life, the bumpier the ride.

I eventually turn around and head back onto the main road and continue on my merry way until I spy another challenging hill on the horizon and psyche myself for another uphill battle.

You know, you could get off the bike and just walk it, my inner Get-Out-of-Jail-FREE card voice says. No one has to know.

Now don't overdo it, Lo; it's been a while since you've ridden at this pace for this long.

I yell "shut up!" to everyone in my head.

I'm thinking, If I build momentum well before the hill's incline, it makes the climb easier, so I flick into top gear and crank it like the kid in the movie E.T. I raise my ultra-padded rump up off the seat, hit "granny" gear and climb up, up, up the hill, peak at the top, then fly down, down, down, which is like crack candy to biking enthusiasts.

I click from one to three on the gear shift while in descent, which allows me to coast for a bit. My legs, butt, abs, and lungs thank me for the reprieve in exertion. The bowels will thank me later ... another bonus of riding.

Don't you think a bicycle's mechanisms are synonymous with our own ups and downs as we tackle life's adversities? It's all about tension. Sometimes we need a lot to get the job done, and other times you just gotta ease on down the road. Riding a bike gives you lots of time to think about things like this.

The asphalt is really roughed up in places, and I skirt those patches as best I can. I sniff the air which reminds me of Mom's freshly laundered sheets on the clothesline in our backyard when we were growing up.

The fields on either side of the road are lush green; the fully matured corn stalks wave at me in the wind as I whiz by. I attune to the sounds in and around me—the bike chain that's making a peculiar click, my heavy breathing, and the wind blowing kisses between the slats of my helmet. I hear a ratty-tat-tat up and look over to my right to spy a red-headed woodpecker sticking its beak where it belongs, foraging for snacks on the outside of a not-long-for-this-world scrub tree.

About ten kilometres into my trek, I stop at the side of the road beneath a large maple and hide out from the intensity of the sun. I pull out the BPA-free water bottle from my pouch and guzzle freely. My eyes slurp in the beauty of the roaming horses in yonder field. The green paint on the barn anchored on the massive property looks fresh, even though the structure itself appears to be in its twilight years. The bright green John Deere tractor and combine look like they were bought as a set to match the rest of the farm.

·Once settled back on my own metal steed, I turn back in the direction of home, feeling lighter and brighter now that my head has done an internal clean-up of its own. I am bathed in a summer slick of sweat. Once again, I stand up on my bicycle for a higher perspective and see that all is right with the world.

I barrel over the pea-sized gravel, pine needles, and cones that litter our driveway like a welcome mat. I come to a halt on the green grass of our front lawn. Dismounting, I groan out the lactic acid in the muscles then bend at the waist and sway back and forth to loosen up the knots and kinks. Standing now, I free the kickstand and walk my bike over to the garage and press the code to open the door.

My guy, John, must have heard the garage door creak. He opens the door from the house and greets me with his sunny smile. "Good ride?" he asks.

"You betcha."

"Lunch is ready – egg salad."

"Be in in a jiffy," I say, peeling off the sunglasses, helmet, and gloves.

I walk my bike to its allotted space at the back of the garage and gather the contents from my pouch. I let out a sudden sigh. Even though everything hurts so good, I believe it's my body's way of high-fiving me, and I high-five it right back with a grateful smile, then head in for some well-earned grub.

Oh, Dear Life

You're a game, a gift, a crazy rat race.
A shit show, a "trip," a slap in the face.
A riddle, a lovefest, a big fucking bore,
A fight to the finish to collect more and more.

We cling to the life raft of things we can lose—
a lover, the job, the grey matter we use.
It's not all the "stuff" that gives life true meaning.
But the light inside is where we should be leaning.

Our world's full of anger, suffering, and pain,
We incessantly judge, ridicule, and complain.
Come on people now, try to love one another,
Your family and friends, global sisters, and brothers.

Our patterns, perspectives, and out-dated beliefs,
Birth our dreams and desires, but also our griefs.
Let the false self be soothed, then loved and adored,
Raise your true Self to prominence as "Head of the Board."

Let go of the past, be quiet, be still.
Check in with your body, surrender your Will.
Old shit will still surface, shake hands, and part friends.
On your Mind's imagination your future depends.

Inside each of us all lies this lost little kid,
Insecure, and scared, their secrets well hid.
The heartaches and boo-boos though never resolved,
Can be healed with compassion when love is involved.

Your first breath arrives on the day you are born,
The start of an oak tree, you're a sweet wee acorn.
Then, poof, one day, just out of the blue,
Your very last breath expels out of you.

"Where did the time go? It went by in a blink,
"Stop the presses," you holler. "I've been hoodwinked!
"My contract's been cancelled, this bloody well bites.
"Call upstairs, I demand my rights!

"I wanted a soulmate, that trip to Peru,
"A purpose, more joy, bigger paycheque – I'm due!
"I've worked my ass off, followed the rules, been good,
'You reap what you sow,' that's what I understood."

But it's far too late now, as the curtain is drawn,
The Universe declares, "It is time to move on."
It asks, "What have you learned on this journey you've endured?
"Would you sign up again for a 'Planetary Life Tour?'"

Heaven's mystery is up, it's been handed to you.
It's all divine timing, yep, right on cue.
So don't be a'scared, there's nothing to resist,
It's a paradise to behold, honest, we insist.

Honk if You Love Laughing

The other day driving around doing errands, I came up behind a big yellow school bus. Standing at the very back of the vehicle, a dewy-faced kid with dark, curly hair waves at me. He looks to be about eleven years old. With a huge grin on my face, I wave back. This little guy laughs at my response, and I see him call to his buddies to join him in the game.

"Here we go." I brace for the middle finger or the tongue and wonder if "mooning" is even a thing anymore. "Sweet little darlings," I think sarcastically, bracing for their juvenile antics.

The lead kid waves again and motions me with a fist pump to honk my horn.

What the hell ... honk, I did. Out came the kid in me, ready to play. He is delighted and motions again. I turn my head away and look busy finding something in my purse to avoid encouraging too much frivolity for one day. I then slowly glance back.

Another car rolls up by the left rear side of the bus and the kid and his posse wave with gusto vying for the attention of the passenger in the car. Again, they try to hail another honk. No dice. The vehicle's passenger looks at its driver, then glances back at the young boys and gives a polite nod.

Little Mr. Determination's eyes lock back onto mine and I shrug. He smiles, which turns on the high beams of my heart.

The traffic light finally turns green and the bus lurches forward. It appears the hot-on-the-toot-trail kid enrolls his friends to let me, the lady in the car behind the bus, know they demand more horn action. Fists and elbows are frantic for some return on their efforts.

"This is ridiculous," I hear the stern voice inside my head, reminding myself of my age.

"Nonsense," my Inner Goof declares. "Never give up an opportunity to play."

As the space between the bus and my car widens, I give the school bus gang my best smile and a thumbs up, then I lay on the horn. Not once, not twice, but three times ... with glee.

I don't have the cajones to look around and observe the reaction of my fellow drivers, so I peel around the bus and take off knowing I made the day of a group of adorable young schoolboys, as well as my own.

Kids can still be kids, no matter what age was my takeaway from this wonderful exchange of kookiness. Thanks, you little rascals.

Enough

All right, enough is enough. Have you had enough of "I'm not enough?"

Where did the aching, proving, climbing, seeking and desperate need to be enough come from anyway?

Is there ever going to be enough "enoughness" to satisfy our "not enough?"

Let's take this so-called "lack of enough," as in, not being pretty, smart, brave, young, perfect, creative, educated, loveable, happy, fulfilled, or ambitious enough, and give it a big kiss and a boot and send it on an extended lifetime holiday.

I know I have had enough of the perceived famine of enough. There is more than enough "enough" to go around. In fact, there are boundless reserves of "enough" to guarantee enough enoughness for infinity.

I am enough. You are enough. We're all enough. Isn't that enough?

Enough already. Are we all agreed?

Good enough!

Ode to Elda

Re-written from a letter I gave my Mother-in-Law for Mother's Day in 2002

I opened the door to my out-of-town refuge. It's just an ordinary space, on the small side, and nothing in particular jumps out at you and says, "look at me, I'm special." But looks can be deceiving.

I approached the bed and pulled down the pink polyester sateen coverlet and folded it neatly at the foot of the queen-sized bed. I grasped the underlying linens and pulled them back, creating an opening for me to slip into. This was my peace and rest sanctuary. I laid my head back on the pillow already dented and wrinkled by another's head and closed my eyes.

I was immediately engulfed by the familiar scent of Dove soap, Downy fabric softener, and just a hint of mothballs. Home Sweet Home. I brought the edge of the top blanket to my nose and inhaled her very essence, separate from any commercial or synthetic smell. It's nothing discernible or definable, but distinctly hers and hers alone. I would have recognized this scent anywhere. It permeated her home and everything in it. Anyone who entered her domain left with a bit of her on them.

I opened my eyes and looked around the room. Simplicity came to mind—gentle pastels, sheers on the window—nothing garish or ostentatious. I took in the simple possessions on the chest of drawers that sat across from the foot of her bed. There was a white plastic statue of Mother Mary, a porcelain bowl with a lid which stored safety pins, orphaned earrings, spare change, and discarded buttons, a heavenly angel figurine, and a dark oak jewellery box that held the rings and gold chains she'd been given or she bought over the years, mostly acquired in Italy. Her most coveted piece, signifying her most coveted role, was the family ring which proudly displayed a birthstone for each of her six children: Rose, Frank, Henry, John, David, and Marlene. Her children had all pitched in and bought it for her.

The walls were painted in a solemn beige tone. Upon them were religious reminders of her devotion to her Maker. Each depiction showed the gentleness of the Madonna, her Child, and his children. They denote love and faith, both words aptly describing everything about this woman.

Elda's son, John, and I married in August 1980 and for the first few years whenever we visited Hamilton, we slept in the basement on a fold-out couch. Elda's husband, Otello, John's dad, died in 1986, having taken his last breath in this very room, on this very bed. John's mom wouldn't hear of us sleeping in the basement anymore on our subsequent visits and insisted we sleep in their master bedroom; she took the spare bedroom. John and I called it the "honeymoon suite"—after we got used to sleeping in the "death bed," of course. It really gave us the creeps for a while.

I called her bedroom my "escape hatch" and made solitary visits there to embrace the blessed quiet when the rest of the house was full of the noise and chaos wrought by her six kids and their kids, the aunts, uncles, cousins, and friends when they all came a-callin'. This family was Italian, after all, so what are ya gonna do? You shutta you face and suck it up.

For over thirty years this woman mothered me, unknowingly perhaps. She provided security, stability, and welcomed me into her fold at a time when my own family life was crumbling. And she fed me, oh boy, did she feed me! John and I started dating when we were seventeen and sixteen, respectively, so she was like my umbrella in the rain when I needed her most.

A more unselfish woman I have never known, and I am truly blessed to have had her in my life. Her strong devotion to God and her family was what defined her. She was a hard-working mother who cared for and served her husband, children, and large extended family with fierce determination. Her office was her kitchen. She spent oodles of time over a hot stove cooking from morning 'til night, tending the massive garden in the summer and harvesting the fruits and vegetables for all to enjoy. She had a wonderful sense of humour and a generous spirit—both shared unconditionally with all she met. You never left her house empty-handed as leftovers were a parting gift to all who sat and dined at her table. This woman could carry on a conversation with anyone, because she had the gift of gab and a huge heart.

I felt at ease and playful with her. Though she was not comfortable with outward displays of affection, I know she loved me. You know how I know? I know because about five years after being married to her son she yelled at me in the kitchen for something I'd done wrong. That's when I knew that I was part of the clan.

She struggled with congestive heart failure for a number of years, which led to her demise, and Elda Partenio Lenarduzzi left this world at the age of seventy-nine, warning her children she would come back and make them pay if they didn't get along after she died. Her biggest worry was the family unit would fall apart, which would break her heart all over again.

Elda has been gone many years now, and the Lenarduzzi family is still the same, but different. Her six kids, now in their fifties, sixties, and seventies, had a total of thirteen children. At this present time, six of her grandchildren have gone on to create nine more little ankle-biters, with more to come ... maybe. Elda's children, Rose, Frank, and Dave are now devoted grandparents themselves, while Henry and Marlene wait patiently for the blessed event. And John and I? Well, we just sit back and enjoy the show from the cheap seats.

I really did have the best Mother-in-Law a girl could ask for, and I count myself super fortunate for being a part of this loving, generous, wackaduzzi bunch.

Now I See

My friend, Leslie, and I have our regular route down pat. A few times a week, we walk the worn paths of Heber Down Conservation area which butts up against Macedonian Village, where my husband John and I live in the town of Brooklin. This tiny hamlet was founded in 1945 by Macedonian families living in Toronto who wanted to escape the big city on weekends and holidays. No two houses are alike here, which makes it unique. Leslie and I try to get out in whatever weather is thrown our way to keep our thighs toned and lips loose.

Angry-looking rain clouds may loom overhead but we gals barely notice as we're too pumped about getting our heart rates up. The sharp autumn air bites our nostrils and cheeks, each breath accelerating as we push ourselves beyond our limits. The rush of anticipatory endorphins will catch up later, which we count on to make this effort all worthwhile.

Towards the end of our one-hour workout, Leslie suggests a shortcut up the steep embankment to shave ten minutes off our time. We've taken it a few times before but today it's a no-brainer because we're freezing our butts off and, more importantly, there's tea and homemade lemon and cranberry muffins waiting for us at my place.

At the base of the embankment is a rotting bog of leaves, logs, and brown icky muck. "Whose bright idea was this?" Leslie asks, her freckly face pinching at the offensive smell.

I offer to take one for the team and go first. I place my right foot, clad in apple-red Nike running shoes, on a slippery log and follow with my left. I pitch forward, arms and legs flailing, trying to right my wrongs while fumbling from one log to the next until I safely hit dry land. "Woo Hoo," I scream, my arms up like two goal-posts. I didn't realize I'd been holding my breath until I pull a deep one in,

76

relieved I'd avoided doing a face-plant in the smelly swamp.

"Your turn, chickipoo," I encourage my dear friend of twenty years. Leslie and I met at a community event for health and wellness; she was a nutritionist and I was a massage therapist. It was a match made in heaven. She lives not too far from me in Port Perry with her honey, Tony.

It's Leslie's turn to venture through the log minefield; she slips once and gets a decent soaker, and I get a good laugh. I offer her a leg-up by way of an outstretched arm and grab her before she lands tits up. From here we scale the embankment and tromp up the path towards home—sweaty and triumphant. Ten feet from my front door, I stop in my tracks. I pat my chest, the top of my head, then the pockets of my puffy poppy-red jacket.

"Shit, my sunglasses," I say, feeling along the collar of my tee-shirt.

"You sure you had them on when we started?" Leslie asks.

"Sure, I'm sure. I thought I'd hooked them in the front of my shirt. Crap! They could be anywhere; we were gone for over an hour." Going back over our route isn't an option, as it's already getting late. I have appointments lined up for a good part of the day—after our tea, of course. I have a lot on my plate of late ... the clinic, the three-month cranial-sacral therapy course I am enrolled in, and then John and I are off to Italy after that. Which means no more walkies for me for a while. "For fuck sakes," I growl.

Seven months later the tulips are stretching their limbs skyward after a long winter's nap. I coerce my husband into taking a walk through the conservation area with me. My plan is to retrace the steps I'd taken with Leslie late in October of the previous year.

My fitness regime with Leslie had come to halt over the winter as Leslie and her partner decided to move to Stouffville, north of Scarborough. I'm bummed my sister-friend has moved, but I can't blame her as she wants to be closer to her family.

I am still upset about losing my fancy frou-frou sunglasses and I'm disappointed in myself for not going back to find them at the time. However, considering what others and the world are dealing with, finding my stupid sunglasses seems silly and trivial. I still mourn their loss but keep it on the QT.

John and I scour the trail last taken, coming up empty-handed. We arrive at the spot that had almost sent us "girls" head-over-heels last year. I bend down to pick up a thick branch which lay among the log orphans—the same ones we'd played hopscotch with to get over to and up the embankment last year. Covering them now are the dead remains of last fall and winter's leftovers, cooked up by Mother Nature herself. I lift the branch high in the air and call up to the heavens, "Calling all angels, please help me find my sunglasses." I begin rooting around in encrusted leaf piles that remind me of phyllo pastry.

John snorts, then rolls his eyes. "Listen, I'm heading home, got things to do. You know, Lo, you have a snowball's chance, heh heh, but carry on. Don't let me stop you. Heh heh." I look up to see him retreat up the steep incline, giving me a brief wave as he heads towards home.

"Oh, ye of little faith, my fine friend," I shout with synthetic confidence in his general direction. My shoulders settle an inch or so lower once John has gone his merry way. This leaves me time to play with my trusty stick, plinking away the old to make way for the new that spring always serves up in her sensuous way.

I take one last stab with the flick of my switch into the mouldy mound, sending dank debris up into the air and splattering it over my face, chest, and arms. I sputter and spit, and brush myself off. I look down at the ground, and there lies a stylish talisman – my prescription Chanel sunglasses.

"Holy shit!" I gasp. Astounded, I lean over to grab my buried treasure for further inspection. They're coated lightly with leaf dust and dirt; I blow away the debris and declare them otherwise unscathed. I'm gobsmacked, my mouth agape with amazement attesting to the fact that I have just witnessed a miracle. I look around to see if I can share my joyous news with anyone but have to settle for the rocks and trees. Eyes to the skies, I whisper, "Thanks, guys."

I sprint up the embankment and run for home as fast as my legs will take me. Winded and wired, I open the front door and call out for my man.

"Oh, Doubting Thomas, guess what I found?"

I sport a smug smirk as I wash my hands in the kitchen sink, I say to myself, "Can't wait to tell, Leslie. She's not going to believe this."

Twenty-eight years later, I still have these sunglasses. I placed them on a shelf where I see them every day, as they serve as a beautiful reminder that miracles happen all the time. Didn't Einstein say something about the idea that we can live our lives either as though nothing is a miracle, or that everything is? I myself choose door number two.

The Merry Old Land of Gah's

"Hello?"

"Is this Mrs. Lenarduzzi?"

"Yes, can I ask who's calling, please?

"Dr. T's office. Results are in—rare spinal condition, blah blah. Surgery required. Yada yada."

I hung up the phone. I stood there and stared. A gush of liquid anguish surged straight for my tear ducts. A reflexive spasm of fear clamped my gut and burned its tender tissue. My stone-cold hand rushed to the spot to soothe the pain. This is the day survival and anxiety took up residence and decided to stay awhile.

After almost a full year, I was still healing from a radical hysterectomy (removal of the whole shebang—uterus, fallopian tubes, and ovaries), and a bowel resection that took out three parts of my large intestine as well as my appendix. All this surgical drama was due to endometriosis, which is a condition resulting from the endometrial tissue straying outside the uterus into other parts of the abdomen causing severe pelvic pain. The Doc sliced from belly button to pubes and tacked it all back together with a staple gun. I was thirty-eight years old. And the best post-surgery gift I received was no more bloody periods! Ha ha, get it?

This, however, was the least of my problems. I had just been informed, via phone call, that I had two serious neurological conditions relating to my brain and spinal cord. Madre de Dios! Prior to the hysterectomy and bowel resection, I was exhibiting numbness in both feet. I saw a neurologist who performed numerous tests to figure out what the cause was, but found nothing. After umpteen medical appointments, they finally decided to book me in for a Magnetic Resonance Imaging (MRI), which was a harrowing experience as I was in that tube for close to two hours. If you've ever had one of these babies, you'll know you have to lay ram-rod still during the scan, and if you are remotely claustrophobic in any way, shape or form, it's a torture chamber. It so happened, I would have episodes of claustrophobia over several years of my lifetime stemming, I believe, from being locked in a bathroom for an hour, trying to get out, when I was four years old. Neither my mother nor her friend, Olga, could unlock the powder room door, so they called the fire department. Two massive firemen loomed before me, once they got the door open, in full get-up with axes raised in their gloved hands; I was scared skinny. I never used Olga's bathroom again after that if Mom and I were invited for coffee.

The contraption they lock in over your head in the MRI machine just adds to the panic, so I take a little pill to put me at ease. Frankly, I think the deep breathing does more to relax me than anything. Post MRI, the radiologist discovered a cyst in my spinal cord which spanned from C1-T11. That's a biggie – from the top of the vertebral column at the back of my head to the bottom of my rib cage, around mid-back. Cat scans and other neuro-related tests followed. Then came the damned X-rays. I spent hours in the X-ray department with the technicians running in and out explaining to me they had to do repeated tests over and over again; I was freaking out not knowing what was happening. When this ordeal was over, I tearfully asked why these x-rays had taken them so long and why so many. One of technicians explained they'd had trouble finding the top of my spinal cord and were quite concerned. Well, I surmised that the MRI Department didn't share their findings with the X-Ray Department, which f-ing pissed me off because if the MRI Department had actually taken the time to communicate their findings, they'd have saved me a whole hell of a lot of x-rays, radiation, and distress.

The results of all this testing, when I got them, shocked the shit out of me.

Diagnosis #1: Syringomyelia—This is a complex disease identified as a syrinx or cyst that forms in the spinal cord. As the cyst fills with cerebrospinal fluid, it expands, putting pressure on the spinal cord. Multiple neurological symptoms are moderate to severe due to nerve damage.

Diagnosis #2: Arnold-Chiari (kee-AH-ree) **Malformation**—

This is an uncommon condition where the brain's cerebellum (which sits at the back of your head and controls coordination and balance) and the brain stem (which connects your brain to your spinal cord and controls automatic functions such as breathing, digestion, heart rate, and blood pressure) both extend into the spinal canal. Signs and symptoms include severe headaches, issues with balance, numbness in the hands or feet, and dizziness, to name a few.

The first neurosurgeon I saw shoved my MRI film results into the illuminated light thingamajig on the wall and declared, "Wow, this is the largest cyst I have ever seen."

He looked me dead in the eye and said, "You have some decisions to make. You'll need surgery, of course. Your life as a massage therapist is finished. That means no more yoga, either. Both put too much stress on the spine."

Fist to the solar plexus.

"But ... how ... what ...? Hot tears begged for release, but I ordered them back.

This slick prick of a man made my skin crawl. He sported a Miss Clairol-tinted coif and two pinky rings. To round out the image, he had dead-shark eyes and a face that got a lot of spa attention. Not once did this doctor smile, give a hint of reassurance, or show any compassion. My ire had been provoked and I responded in that hateful quivery voice I get when I'm scared or facing conflict with an authority figure.

"How would you feel if someone just told you that you would never practice neurosurgery again?" I asked.

"Well, Mrs. Lenarduzzi," he replied smugly, "if it came down to my career versus my life, then I'd have no choice now, would I?"

His chin dared me to top that one. *Fucking asshole.* I caved and became the submissive good little patient; I didn't have much fight left in me, quite frankly.

I got my petty revenge, though, not that the guy gave a flying fadoo, but I found another more caring, empathetic doctor who I simply adored from the first moment we met: Dr. Charles Tator. He reminded me of the beloved TV doctor, Marcus Welby, MD. A mop of white hair helped me place him in his late sixties and he had a gentle smile that reached his eyes.

With a vengeance I followed a nutrient-rich diet, meditated daily, practiced yoga (despite what that dick doctor said) and read uplifting books. I was massaged, reiki'd, crystalled and counselled. You name it, I tried it, hoping to calm my fried nervous system.

I entered Toronto Western Hospital a few months later at peace with whatever the outcome of the operation might be. I truly felt in a good place with God and was prepared to let him/her handle the details.

I awoke in the Intensive Care Unit (ICU) with what felt like a hatchet embedded in the back of my skull. The surgical ordeal was over but the pounding in my head wasn't. They'd split open the occipital bone at the back of my skull to relieve the pressure from the parts that were pressing into my spinal cord and brain stem. Part of this process was the removal of a section of the bone at the back of the skull. This surgery was called a "posterior fossa decompression," designed to right the wrongs going on inside my cranium (not the juicy ones though, ha ha) and stop the symptoms from getting worse. The neurosurgeon had used a part of the tensor fascia lata muscle on the outside of my left thigh to glue my cranial bones back together. I like to say I gave my head a "leg up."

There was an operation to help drain the cyst/syrinx by way of a stent in the case of Syringomyelia, but the results were varied, according to my neurosurgeon. Because of the Arnold-Chiari condition I also had, he didn't encourage it. Some patients having this surgery ended up with severe disabilities and more neurological problems than before, so this was not an option for me.

The staff at Toronto Western Hospital were at my beck and call throughout the five days I spent in ICU. Once I moved to a private room (thank you Ontario Power Generation—John's place of work), flowers, cards, and well-wishers arrived.

Post-surgery was no picnic. Moving my head was torture so I kept a cold, wet washcloth draped over the top of my throbbin' noggin' and maintained a statue-like stillness. And the drugs, oh, the glorious drugs, were my closest friends for just a little while.

After a few days, I wailed to my husband, John, "Wouldn't you think if someone is lying in bed after major surgery with a wet rag slapped over their face, people might get the hint and make their visit short and sweet?" Not a chance. John and I both come from families of six kids. He's Italian and I am as Canadian as Canadian can be. I pleaded for a minimum of people to visit—parents and sib-lings only. During that first week my parents and four of my five brothers came. Then the Italians arrived by the numbers; in this cul-ture "no" means "yes." Then the friends followed—from high school, work, and the neighbourhood. I felt obliged to stay awake during everyone's stay, when all I wanted to do was sink into oblivion. I sobbed the minute guests left—a heaving, gulping, snot-sodden cry that clamped a holy wrench around my poor swollen melon.

During the week that followed, I said to John, "I'm exhausted from telling people the same G-D story over and over again. I can't handle any more visitors."

"But people are calling and wanting to come see you. What am I supposed to tell them?" John replied.

I shook my head a little too rigorously, which I paid for. "No more company; I know they mean well, but, once I get home and I feel stronger, then I can see them." Feelings of guilt tore into me, but I refused to cave in to being the "good girl" – making other peo-ple happy or comfortable, at my own expense. Going through this traumatic time in my life taught me the power of saying, 'no," for the sake of my own well-being.

As weeks went by my strength returned in bits and spurts. I was so happy to be home. I'd just turned forty years old but felt I'd lived eighty. Shuffling up and down the driveway was an aerobic workout, but I was grateful to be walking as others with this con-dition are not so lucky. Simple things were a momentous cause for celebration—making myself tea and toast and showering were like bread to a starving man.

Five months into my healing process, I was able to turn my head forty-degrees each way, though I had minimal forward and backward extension. My head and shoulder muscles were like bands of Indian rubber, which I swaddled in colourful scarves to keep warm and protected. I was stiff but stylin'. The seven-inch incision was healing nicely according to Dr. Tator. I was thrilled to be back walking in the conservation area that backed onto the little hamlet I lived in. I still co-owned a massage therapy clinic in downtown Whitby, so I went in a few days a week to attend to business but was allowed no hands-on work. It felt so good to be more like "me" again.

My expectations of myself, my relationships, my business, our home, and our life were all lofty. I would get a "high" on the sheer adrenaline rush I got from planning, organizing, fixing, and running my (our) life. I was addicted to the "buzz." I did everything at break-neck speed. My lifetime pattern of running non-stop was a tough one to break. My head was going a mile a minute, but my body wasn't willing to play. "Hmm, balance problems? Perhaps there was a pattern here?"

I began a gentle yoga practice, as I had taught yoga prior to my diagnosis. "Screw him," I thought back to the first dweeby neuro-surgeon I'd seen. Upstairs in the spare room, I was downward dog-ging and as I came up from the down, planet Earth tumbled out of gravity's embrace and took me with her. My eyes were unable to focus on any one spot in the room, and the floor that had once held me upright fell open like a trapped door and down I went onto the clutches of the abyss. I bleated out loud to no one's ears. John was at work. The room continued to flip and flop like a kite gone rogue in a gale-force wind. My hands creepy-crawled along the wall to stabilize the body that no longer felt like mine. A foul stench from my armpits assaulted my nasal passages which was a clue that my nervous system was on high alert, telling the rest of my body to ding-ding-ding, "break a leg, emergency here!"

I bum-walked down the stairs to the phone and called my husband to come home.

I spent two terrifying months in bed recovering from this post-surgery trauma. Vertigo was slowly sucking the life from me like dirty dishwater down a semi-clogged drain. I no longer felt sure of anything anymore; this was a double dip into the survival pool. The only thing I could do was surrender and let go. Life became a series of small victories: getting myself to the bathroom, cleaning a sink, or making a sandwich. How we take little everyday actions for granted.

It was a humbling, crippling, debilitating time in my life—

though, not knowing it at the time, it came laden with gifts.

My dear sweet husband became chief cook, nursemaid, and sole breadwinner. You really find out the fabric with which your marriage is woven when adversity comes a-callin'. His love and devotion to me were undeniable.

After the worst of the worst was over and I was on the road to recovery again, I could tell I was progressing because I was getting antsy. My business partner and I disbanded the massage therapy clinic. I was too ill, and she was too pregnant. I felt lost without a cause, identity, or label to define me. I was stripped clean, exposed, and vulnerable. I was always a "something"—a student, an assistant, an office manager, a sales rep, a massage therapist.

When I showed up in new social situations, people would ask that stupid, lame question, "So, what do you do?" This would trigger my insecurity and newfound non-status which made the defenses come out with their dukes up. My confidence was shaky; my energy, having been once bitten, was twice shy. These days, semi-to-severe vertigo taunted my psyche, and I lived in fear of losing my place in the world again. I felt unsafe in my body, like someone forgot to flick the "fight and flight" button to the "off" position. I continued to have symptoms of paresthesia (an abnormal sensation of tingling or prickling) and numbness in both lower extremities and in my hands, not to mention the freakin' anxiety that rattled my timbers, the muscle pain and contractions, digestive issues, and postural imbalance. My body was constantly surprising me with something new. The muscles in my thighs, calves, back, and neck were tight and contracted, and I had to widen my stance when I walked, otherwise I'd walk like I'd had a few too many and feared toppling over. The anxiety sure didn't help my digestion at all. I had to watch what I ate so it wouldn't cause pain or inflammation. So, goodbye gluten, so long dairy. My journal absorbed much of my anger, fear, and frustration.

If I had a dollar for every "fuck" I recorded ...

I gave myself permission to feel all my outrage and despair and to spit the toxic venom I was feeling out onto the page. Cathartic emotional releases in the form of ugly cries were part of the bonus package, and I decided not to resist or stop them. A journal can be one of the best friends you'll ever have; all you need is a pen and a dollar-store writing tablet. Mine sits patiently on my bedside table waiting for me to converse with it, as I have done almost every morning for thirty years. Thankfully, it doesn't judge, censor, or correct my spelling or grammar. Even better, it doesn't text nor interrupt while I'm talking, or listen with half an ear. I let whatever is going on inside of me rip, and I record it on the page. Writing down your true-blue feelings, emotions, thoughts, and ideas gives the mind something to do, which leaves space for visions, insights, aha moments, and eurekas. You'll be tempted to poo-poo, negate, dissect, and analyze the shit out of this process because, typically, that's what we tend to do as human beings. But we can't, because these inspirational messages come from the highest aspect of ourselves: our creative intelligence. Many people have no idea what this is or even feels like, but just ask an artist, musician, or writer; these gifts come from the great beyond, often through us acting as conduits.

I've come to realize we humans are not comfortable expressing negative emotions, though thinking them is as common as breathing. Expressing how we really feel? Are you kidding? What would people think? What would happen if we did? Good God!

My health continued to throw me a few curve balls and I had to sit it out for a few innings, but I got back in the game. Not the same game, though. I chose to paint myself a new life in creative self-expression. My creativity began to voice itself, begging for some attention and expression, once my life had been stripped of all I felt was normal.

"Huh? Me? Creative?"

Ya, ya sure, I could decorate a room, plan menus, cook, put together a dinner party, throw together a Lois-look from my closet, blah blah blah. My creativity was crying out for more—far more. It began with the journal writing, which greased the wheels of courage and inspiration. Then came the poems and stories. Once the creative floodgates opened, new ideas flowed in, unleashing the higher expression of who I was meant to be. I locked onto the idea of gathering women together for a Play Day designed with fun and freedom in mind. It was the medicine I needed to get my mind off my troubles. It was a joy to organize a day of meditation, writing, improv, movement, interactive games, and organic facials. It went over very well! The only thing missing, I felt, was an artsy-fartsy project.

Art therapy was becoming more popular at the time in the psychotherapy world and I was curious to explore it, so I did some research prior to my next planned Play Day workshop. Armed with a smattering of knowledge, and new brushes, paints, and canvases, I became my own guinea pig and tried out the art therapy exercise on myself. It was both fun and introspective, and resulted in the very first painting I had ever done as an adult. The last one I had done was in Grade 7. The next full-day workshop, which included the art therapy painting exercise, was a huge success with the ladies. My "pearls" in these workshops was "let go and lose control." Some participants could, others struggled.

The phoenix rising was the therapeutic painting I did for myself. I became giddy with each new paint colour, medium, and technique I explored. What a blast, what a thrill! Out of the ashes, new babies were born ... newborn paintings I birthed myself, as both a creative mother and a midwife. Each of the hundred or so paintings I've done to date has brought up every stinkin' bug-a-boo you can think of (I suck, this isn't good enough, it has to be perfect, etc.), as well as wonderful feelings of accomplishment, excitement, and devotion to the gifts I continue to unwrap. I encourage myself to play with canvas sizes, paint colours, themes, and textures until I come to a gut-feel completion of a piece. After listening to artists both in person and on various social media platforms these past twenty years, I've learned there isn't an artist out there who hasn't struggled with being hard on themselves. Feeling worthy, confident, talented enough, and unique comes with time, practice, and experience in the art world. The trick is to sit your ass in the chair, hunker down, and start. Just do it; whatever it is you yearn to create. Procrastination and insecurity are the gremlins who will eat away at your dreams.

It takes courage to put yourself and your art out there on display for all to see. A thick skin is paramount because people, "God bless their pointed little heads," as my Grandma Penhale used to say, rarely hold back their opinions of your work. You have to paint, write, dance, and sing for YOU ... no one else. I was scared stiff the first time my art went up in a gallery; then I had my first solo show. With each new exposure of my work, I grew stronger

within my Self and in what I was creating. Letting go of other people's approval comes with time, but it's not always easy.

Many of my paintings are an outward expression of the very
stories you will read here in this book. (See "Warrior Woman" on
page 94.) It's much easier to hide your thoughts, beliefs, feelings,
and emotions within brushstrokes on a canvas than it is through
written words on a page. But I promised myself to live life
unapologetically and write from deep within.

As a kid, I coasted to get by, seldom taking risks or putting myself "out there" as I was so afraid of looking dumb, or being laughed
at, criticized, or judged. I never took art beyond middle school or
sang in a choir, nor had I written anything more meaningful than a
book report. I was a Nervous Nellie who dreaded being called on by
the teacher, as I mentioned previously. You'd have to make me beg
for my life or pay up big time before I'd raise my hand in class.

Life has a way of helping you grow a spine, however, and that's
why God outfitted me with five wild and crazy brothers, a strait-
laced, conservative mother, and a fun-loving, freedom-seeking dad.
It's all paved the way for me to become feisty, sweetly-warped, *me*.
"Nobody is the boss of me," was, is, and always will be a well-versed
line of mine. Over time, I have whittled away at the "crusty" defensive armour this mantra has provided in the past, and softened it to,
"I teach people how to treat me." Towards the end of high school,
the pressure was on to decide what each student wanted to "be"
when they grew up. I had little ambition to "be" anything, other
than free. I got a full-time job after college and moved out of the
house a year later, once I had saved up enough money. That was the
beginning of "coming into myself" on this road to self-mastery and
independence. I'm working on a Lifetime Achievement Award in
this category. *Good luck with that, Lo.*

That comfort zone we like to inhabit isn't all it's cracked up to be. It
can also be a cage around myriad creative possibilities waiting to ignite
passion and joy from within the same-old, same-old routines that often
make up our everyday life. I am determined to get out there and play
with wild abandon as I paint, write, sing, dance, and drum. One of the
biggest creative projects I encouraged myself to try, as I mentioned in

another one of my stories, was to co-write a comedic variety show with three other women; we called ourselves *The Rack Pack*. Now that was a humdinger of a dare, but I got up on stage, acted, and sang to prove to the little girl inside of me—who had been too freaked out to expose herself so many years ago—that I could do it. I put my all into it and had a blast. I was pretty green and unseasoned, but I ticked it off my "gotta do" list with pride. Every creative endeavour I have poured myself into causes my insecurities to rise to the surface, but these are just old habitual loops of thoughts and beliefs running willy-nilly in my head from the past. They eventually lose steam once I have built up my creative confidence.

I continue to have neurological symptoms, balance issues, and acute vertigo off and on (and well, hello ... let's not forget my ol' friend, anxiety), but those years of extreme turmoil are behind me. They created one of the hardest, most stressful points in my life, but I came through it with some spectacular parting gifts related to creative self-expression.

I have gained incredible wisdom and knowledge over the years that cannot be ordered or bought. The time to search, explore, and discover myself were handed to me on a silver platter. This is an ongoing process, of course, but I have earned a PhD in life skills with no degree or certificate to show for it, other than the one imprinted in my cellular memory.

My intention from this current vantage point is to spend my remaining years kick-assing life as I wake up, shake up, loosen up, open up, and speak up into the highest version of myself—healthy, strong, fulfilled, and fabulous.

Wanna join me?

You can't have made it to this stage of the game without getting bulldozed over by a Mack truck or two along the way. Many of my close friends and family members have scaled the arduous and pain-ful walls of divorce, the loss of a child or a spouse, the death of par-ents or siblings, and serious health issues.

Luckily, the timing of adversity in my life has always been in my favour and I've observed that, more often than not, shit-storms set up camp at different times for different people so friends and family members can be there to catch you when you fall. This is a reciprocal arrangement. However, COVID-19, that little dickens, threw a monkey wrench into this arrogant, hair-brained idea that everyone takes turns facing life's hardships and heartache. Our entire global family was hit hard by this viral shit-storm, and we had no way of controlling anything other than our thoughts and reactions to everyone and everything, and the self-care we took on for ourselves and our loved ones.

My husband went over and above the call of duty in honouring his vows to me, "in sickness and in health." You sure know who your true-bluers are when life up-ends your apple cart and you fall into a pit of despair. My dear ones picked me up during the lowest of my lows, bathed me, shampooed me, consoled me, and fed me. What I know in my heart ferly-sherly is that I've come out wiser from every pitfall I've fallen into. The Life Crap that settled on the surface provided the ideal opportunity to assess what was going on in my life." The questions:

What's wrong with me?
Why can't I heal?
What else can go wrong with my body?
Am I going to die?
Am I settling for mediocre or safe or am I willing to unlock my own mental cage?
What am I going to do to shake things up?
What am I scared to face?
Am I truly happy in life, my marriage, where I live?

They're all ones I've wrestled with, and still do, as many have.

Inside my head, those old beaten-down roads I've travelled of limiting patterns, opinions, programs, and perceptions remind me of a needle getting stuck on a 33-rpm record causing it to skip until you can't take it anymore and you are forced to nudge the needle.

"I'm not safe" and "I'm not good enough" have been perpetual pains in my proverbial ass. They were instilled within my sweet innocent psyche from a very young age; I either inherited them or made my own assumptions and believed them to be true. For half my life, I didn't even realize these inner voices were running the show. The limitations in our life are self-created. Upon my studies of the quantum soup we live in, I have read that "the universe does not know whether the vibration you emit (and we do emit an energetic frequency) is because of something you're observing, something you're remembering, or something that you're imagining. It just receives the vibration and answers it with things that match it." Another way of thinking about it is, "the universe is not punishing you, it is simply responding to the vibrational attitude you are emitting." Scary, cool, huh? I realized the negative effect these thoughts had created in my life and I became more aware of the circumstances, events, and people that showed up reflecting these cheeky little beliefs; I set out to be mindful of what I was thinking. By controlling the thoughts you think and how you respond to what shows up in your life by way of circumstances and events, you become the orchestrator of your own life. When you focus your mind on a personal desire or dream, and call up the feelings it will instill in you as if it has already happened, extraordinary gifts will start to appear within your life.

Here's a for-real example ... When I moved to Brooklin, I went looking for a choir to sing with—singing has always given me a high. I searched everywhere on the Web, and asked everyone I could think of and I came up with bupkis. Weeks later, my friend, Jan, popped by for tea and a gab. In the middle of a sentence, she held an index finger up, gently instructing me to stop talking, which I did. "I have a message coming through for you, Lo." Cool. Yes, I have some pretty "out there" friends who have magical gifts, and I'm never one to pass on a gift if it's handed to me. "They tell me you should join a singing group; it would be really good for you," said Jan. *Huh? How do they know I am looking for one*, I thought. "They," meaning, those mysterious universal life forces working on my behalf. I told Jan I had been looking for a choir for some time but hadn't been successful. Five minutes after Jan left, I got a phone call. I had set up a meeting at my home that evening with Anita, the woman who was calling. She told me she needed to cancel as something had come up. "Not a problem; we can reschedule," I said. "You got a hot date tonight?" "No, actually, I want to go check out a new women's choir in Oshawa called, 'Shout Sister.' The first practice starts tonight. There was an article posted in last night's newspaper." I started to giggle and she said, "What's so funny?" I told her of the celestial message I received via my friend, Jan, not five minutes prior, and her wild and wonderful part in delivering the timely message. She was wowed too—"I guess you're supposed to sing, huh?" The funny thing is, Anita never did show up that night for practice, nor ever. A coinkydink?—I think not. I believe those guides and angels working behind the scenes like to play with us, and I'm all in. I was part of that amazing singing group, "Shout Sister," for over ten years, and loved every minute of it.

These days I am learning to lead with my heart, issuing a directive to have my head take a backseat. Learning to put self-care first is uncharted, unfamiliar terrain and it's often hard to navigate, especially when you have people in your life who trigger your shit. You know it's not about them, right? It's about listening "within" to what "feels" expansive in every situation and confrontation, which can feel like walking a tightrope. You're wobbly, scared, and uncertain, but you have a best friend that will help you along the way: your body. It doesn't lie. It will tell you through the sensations you feel whether you are headed for the safety platform or about to take a tumble off the highwire.

Listening to my body and honouring my heart's calling has been one of the greatest gifts I've given myself. It has left me feeling more empowered, ecstatic, and free. Yes, you may face backlash from others who consider your actions selfish when you don't follow the status quo or family or societal traditions and expectations. Yet, there is an undeniable surge of pride that strengthens your resolve when you stand up and stay true to yourself. Learning to say "yes" to yourself and "no" when it feels like a no (or a "no thank you" or "nope, I'm not feeling that's right for me") is a step towards being who you came here to be and living your best and truest life.

Have You Ever Wondered, Woman?

Written and performed by Lois Howard Lenarduzzi for the "Rack Pack Show" in 2013

Heels, Makeup, Bras, And Boys.
Goodbye Braces, Teddy bear, Toys.

Wife, Mother, Daughter, Whore.
I Am Woman, Hear Me Roar.

Bitchy, Bored, Tired, And Spent.
I Need Some Time to Scream And Vent.

Kids Have Left, Popped This Stand.
Sweet Freedom Begins, Now, Ain't It Grand?

I Look In The Mirror, Who's That I See?
Oh My God, That Can't Be Me!

Be Bold And Brave, It's Time To Grow.
Honey, It's You That's Running Your Show.

Now Clamp On Your Bracelets, And Do Some Good.
Be Your Own Superhero, Like Wonder Woman Would.

Mid-Century Re-Model

Chapter One – Birthday Bumps

My fiftieth kick-at-the-can here on Mother Earth is just around the corner. My birthday is June 9th and I've got plans—big plans! Nothing concrete as yet, but I know I want something that's going to blow my skirt up. It has to be challenging, fun, and maybe a little scary to shake things up a bit. I envision a solo trip, just me, myself, and I—no friends, family, or husband.

My husband, John, insists we throw a party.

"Lame," I reply sarcastically, with a devilish grin.

"We have to have a party. This is your big one, a half-century."

"Nope. I mean, no thanks," I reply.

"Why not?"

"I hate birthday parties. They're a snore-fest."

You know the ones. They follow a predictable pattern ... superficial blah blah conversations, a shuffle up to the food table to fill your pie hole, open gifts no one really needs, blow out the candles, the call for "speech, speech," then ya high tail it outta there as fast as you can (after having checked your timepiece for the past hour.)

"It's about getting everyone together." John insists.

"Kids' parties are fun. Let's have one of those. At least there's music, crafts, bouncy castles, and Pin-The-Tail-On-The-Donkey."

"Don't worry, I got this. You don't have to do a thing," John assures me.

I think, *I really wish we could skip the whole party thing.*

I want to do something I've never done before. Well, no bungee jumping, scuba diving, or jumping out of a plane. If this milestone year is going to be a gamechanger, it's up to me to make it happen. Stepping out of the same-old, same-old, forgetting the emphasis on the "old," is my priority. It's my mission to start the search for a bigger, brighter, bolder me.

It begins in February, when my girlfriend, Jennifer H., posts on Facebook about an upcoming one-week retreat she's holding in Bimini—a small island in the Bahamas—to swim with dolphins in the wild. Jennifer is an expert on getting "Unstuck," meaning, she helps people "get out of their own way" of limiting stories, beliefs, and patterns, which ultimately leads to more fulfillment and meaning in their lives. On many of her experiential worldwide adventures, people's greatest fears arise. Her life's work is about assisting others to go beyond their fears, doubts, and foibles so they can achieve quantum-leap results in all areas of life—body, mind, relationships, business, and abundance. Jennifer believes we come here to catalyze through the contrast that shows up in our lives, not coast in sameness, predictability, and conformity. Her partner, Joe, is a professional diver gifted with a heightened sense of connection with the sea world, specifically with whales and dolphins.

I am hell-bent on signing up for this trip-of-a-lifetime but shitting my pants at the prospect. I am terrified to get on a plane for fear that I will have a full-blown vertigo episode. I used to really get a kick out of flying. I have lived with this son-of-a-bitch condition since it showed up a few months after I had head surgery about a decade ago. Just turning my head can literally bring me to my knees, panic attack in tow. I call Joe bawling my face off saying I want to go to Bimini but am shaking in my boots. He soothes me with kind words and says, "Lois, there are always options." He informs me there are three people signed up for the trip who are driving to Fort Lauderdale from Toronto, and he put me in touch with them.

After contacting them, the four of us arrange to leave on April 13th. One of the women offers her vehicle for the trip south. Sasha, the only male in the bunch, can't drive because he has epilepsy. I am comforted by how these angels show up in my life and now I can relax ... until I can't. Two people bail at the last minute, and one decides to fly down on her own. I am angry and frustrated and lost as to what to do.

Sasha calls me and says, "Lois, Joe explained your situation to me. I will go with you however you choose. I won't leave you stranded. Tell me what you want to do."

"Well, I'm looking at bus schedules. There's a Greyhound bus from Toronto to Fort Lauderdale. It's a long trip, though. Then I want to catch a short flight from Fort Lauderdale over to Bimini. It takes only twenty-five minutes, then I'll see how I do with the vertigo."

"Ok, let's do it," Sasha says, and we make our plans. April finally arrives, along with our departure date.

John drops me off two blocks from the bus station in downtown Toronto. A marathon is taking place and many streets have been cordoned off for the event. I give my honey a quick peck on the cheek, then drop and roll with suitcase in hand. I weave between the disgruntled runners, hoofing it to get to the bus on time. My poor husband doesn't even get to meet the man I am going to spend the next week with. Hell, I don't even know what the guy looks like. But once I see Sasha's silly grin looking my way as I run towards the bus that is waiting to be boarded, I recognize him right away.

The gruelling stop-go, stop-go Greyhound voyage takes forty-five hours in total, which gives Sasha and me plenty of time to get acquainted. He is a beautiful thirty-three-year-old walking hormone. Honestly, he oozes sensuality and is quite the charmer to members of the female species ... this one included.

The bus pulls off at a roadside diner somewhere in North Carolina, and the forty passengers climb down and shuffle into the restaurant. Sasha and I sit at a table for two with our beverages and muffins, and the "boy" looks me in the eye and says, "You know, Lois, what happens in Bimini stays in Bimini." Gulp.

"Nice line. Just make that up?" I ask.

I wonder if he is flirting with me or just yanking my chain. I change the subject as it feels like I'm playing with matches around a propane tank. My nether regions, however, are not ignoring his flattery. My body is all aflutter like a sixteen-year-old's reaction to her first boy-crush.

For the duration of the bus trip south we share our life stories, and discover we are both a couple of "head cases"—Sasha with epilepsy and me with vertigo. We sleep the latter part of the journey due to exhaustion.

I have no issues on the tin-can-sized plane we take from Fort Lauderdale to our tiny island destination in the Bahamas. I am grateful for my new friend as he holds my hand during this harrowing experience; my crazy anxiety level evaporates as we start our descent. I now feel prepared to face the flight back to Toronto alone at the end of this crazy escapade.

I drink in Bimini upon landing. It is a small, rustic island; no five-star hotels here. This little patch of paradise looks barely touched by the tourist industry's looky-looers, contrary to most island getaways. Walking the crunchy beach requires full foot gear as it is twelve inches deep with sun-bleached seashells.

The Biminites are quiet, respectful, and friendly people. I feel honoured to share their tropical isle—population 2,500—if only for a short time. Fishing is their mainstay of commerce in case you want to know.

Our host and retreat facilitator, Jennifer, organizes the fourteen attendees on this adventure, all from different parts of Canada and the U.S., into small pods and assigns them their living quarters for the week. For some insane reason, she has me billeted with Sasha.

"What the hell, Jenn? Can't we change the accommodation? This makes me very uncomfortable."

"Arrangements are already set, Lo Lo. You just spent an eternity with him on the bus, so what's the problem?" she laughs.

The outside of our quaint hobbit-sized dwelling is whitewashed and encased in seashells which glimmer with the sun's reflection. Inside, there is a bedroom with a queen-size bed; off the bedroom is a compact living space consisting of a fold-down Chesterfield and a chair. No television, no Wi-Fi, no radio.

Well, I know where I'm sleeping, I think. Sasha makes it clear he's open to sharing the bed; I'm not. I tell him I'm uneasy with this arrangement and point him to the sofa.

This little mitchy-match thing going on between my roommate and me has me on high alert. I haven't felt this overwhelmed with pubescent sexual yearning for a very long time and it scares and exhilarates me at the same time. My husband and I have been together since we were sixteen and seventeen, and we'd hit a drought in this department after twenty-eight years of marriage. Sasha has re-awakened a sleeping Aphrodite.

The first day of our tour begins with introductions and a review of the itinerary, then we mosey on down to a forty-foot boat with instructions to climb aboard. We are introduced to the captain who begins sharing the safety rules of the water and his vessel. The seventeen of us gather and Jennifer asks if we have any questions. What's coming up for each of us? Did any of us have any reservations or concerns?

The boat heads out to sea at a good clip and after a three-and-a-half-hour voyage on the Atlantic, the intensity of the heat and sun has made a bunch of us ready to dive overboard. Finally, we are told to don our wetsuits, masks, snorkels, and flippers—all required gear for this nautical trip. Jennifer and Joe give directions in the art of snorkelling and deep diving, then invite us to enter the vast watery expanse before us. A few keeners jump in with relish, while some slip in gingerly, taking it slow and easy until they get their sea legs. I am part of Team Tentative; even though I can swim, I'm not a super-strong swimmer, and this is a big-ass body of water. Two terrified women cling to the back of the boat's rails, no doubt rethinking their signature on the contract's dotted line. Jenn and Joe's patience and compassionate guidance help one of the ladies with an intense water phobia. By day three, Joe has her deep-dive spear fishing. Oh, to see her face light up with pride and joy when she surfaces with a fish on the end of her spear; it's a miracle to behold.

The second of the two uncertain women screws up the courage to submerge herself into the deep Bimini blue ocean, though she stays close to the boat. Baby steps, eh? Like me and my rinky-dink plane ride here.

It takes a few days to master holding my breath long enough to dive to a depth of fifteen-to-twenty feet, which is where the oceanic art really starts. At first, I get about five feet down, panic, then claw my way back up for heavenly air. Once safe, I look around to see if my dignity has survived. It seems everyone is busy with their own challenges.

The promise of swimming with the dolphins is now a dream about to come true for all of us. Joe calls the dolphins—not a shout-out, but a call out to them from within, which is a curious mystery to the group. Except for the Nervous Nellies, we all hang out in the Atlantic, thirty or so feet from the boat. We are told to keep our arms at our sides so we don't startle the spotted dolphins. Our flippers and wetsuits keep us stationary, afloat, and relatively still as we anxiously await their arrival. This is not a guaranteed outcome, we are told. Our heads and necks crane in all directions searching for the whereabouts of these adorable sea creatures.

I like to think they feel our longing and excitement because within ten minutes they surprise us with their loving presence. We submerge under water and hold our breath with anticipation. My serotonin levels duke it out with my adrenaline levels as I witness and embody this "high" of a lifetime. These fascinating mammals dip and dive all around us; bubbles arise creating a curtain between us and them. Once the bubbles settle, I'm gobsmacked when my eyes meet theirs, making me want to reach out and cop a cuddle, but we have been told this is a no-no. I wonder if their squeaks and clicks are a gossip session. Are they sharing with one another their thoughts of us two-legged, be-goggled creatures?

It's day four of our five-day trip, and after a light breakfast and brief check-in with the gang, we are back frolicking in the mighty Atlantic. Jennifer waves me over to join her and as I get closer, she yells, "follow me," and I happily comply. Big breath in, down, down we go, and my eyes collect the beauteous underworld of fish and coral, all the while keeping my attention on where Jenn is leading me. I register my lung capacity for preservation purposes, but my friend waves me a little further and I kick my fins up a notch. This is when I spy with my little eye, a seven-foot shark.

"Motherfucker," I bellow silently. Arms and legs flailing about wildly, I make my way toward the surface. About halfway up, I meet a barracuda who is only three feet from me; its sinister smile dares me to come closer. I make haste up to where the sun shines, ripping my snorkel and mask off as I come up for air, spewing and spitting my outrage.

"You bitch! You did that on purpose," I scream at Jenn, as she herself surfaces, laughing her fool head off.

"Ah, Lo Lo, it was only a nurse shark. They don't go for hu-mans—well, hardly ever," she teases. Remnants of hysteria still cling as I tell her about the encounter with the barracuda, and her laugh becomes a high-pitched cackle.

That evening we head into the small nearby town for a tasty treat that Jennifer and Joe have arranged for our group. Two fisher-men make us homemade conch salad—a first for most of us. First, they crack open the conch shell with a machete, then they dig out the tender, white meat, and chop it into bite-sized pieces. They add onions, sweet red pepper, and vinegar. It is a sensational feast for the tongue after broiling in the sun and surf all day. Lying in bed that night, it occurs to me that I am being tested big time. "Another fear faced today," I whisper with a smile on my face.

By the end of the week, the lot of us are both ship and soulmates. We are tanned and tired, but also whirling from our heady days of fun and excitement. Now it is time to say our "see-ya-soons and let's-keep-in-touches."

The day before everyone leaves, I decide there is no way in Hell I'm leaving this place, especially after the forty-five-hour slog it took to get here. I inquire at the rental office about extending my stay another week and they offer me a tiny cottage, which is perfect. The kink in the hose is that Sasha has chosen to stay too, on my dime of course. He's not currently employed due the grand mal seizures he's experienced in the recent past. He insists he wants to fly back to Toronto with me, just to make sure I'm okay, which is thoughtful. Jennifer's twinkly eyes and wicked smirk want to know what the hell is going on between the two of us, as she pulls me aside. I break down and divulge the details of the high school crush vibes Sasha and I are exchanging. It's tantalizing and tortuous to feel such intense buried sexual desire. I have a choice to make – "do 'im or don't" and live with the consequences. Jennifer is very supportive and reminds me that our biggest hurdles and fears often come up on these types of trips. She herself left a stable, loving marriage for a lover and other higher callings, and commiserates with my conflict.

Sasha and I cohabitate in the shoebox-size cottage with the mint green siding for another week. It comes complete with two single beds, thankfully, a bathroom, and a tiny kitchen area with a hot-plate, kettle, and coffee pot. It is uncomfortably comfortable, if that's even a thing.

Jennifer and Joe have booked another week in order to chill out after the organized retreat, for which I am relieved. They are staying in a place a ten-minute walk from ours. I've decided they will be both our tour guides and chaperones in case I need one. The four of us spend the week swimming, snorkelling, sightseeing, and cooking meals together. Jenn saunters over to our little Shangri-la one evening and Sasha mixes up some tropical drinks. None of us are tried and true drinkers. On goes the music and we set the night on fire with our dance moves and released inhibitions. Probably not the wisest choice to mix alcohol in with the steaming chemical soup bubbling between my roomy and me.

Sasha is a born romantic and over the week he tries to entice me to let my guard down and release my inhibitions. He had alluded to engaging in Tantric sex in his love life during one of our Greyhound gab sessions. Protective shields up, I stave off this young man's practised carnal moves in this age-old dance of seduction. I bring this climax to a close because in the end I choose to honour my thirty-three-year relationship (twenty-eight years married and five dating) with my husband. I have too much love and respect to tarnish our many years together by having a tawdry affair with a thirty-three-year-old. Sasha is a dear soul, but I surmise from some of the stories he's shared with me that the boy may have some sexual addiction issues. Besides, I'd be heartbroken if the shoe was on the other foot, and there's no way I'm going to let guilt lasso me for life. What this situation has really highlighted is that my libido isn't quite dead yet, it has just been hibernating. I've been through several years of recuperating from major surgeries and sexual intimacy was put on the back burner. In fact, it was locked in a cupboard somewhere. What I deeply desired from this situation, I decided, was a renewed passionate love affair with John, and I have Sasha to thank for this.

I book Toronto-bound, Air Canada flights home for my new buddy and me. I experience a mixed-pickle jar of emotions on the plane. I feel guilt, sadness, anxiety, and excitement, while my vertigo remains steady-eddy, I am thrilled to report. My dear, sweet husband is awaiting my arrival at the gate with an armful of red roses when we land at Toronto Pearson. His beautiful welcome smile blows my heart wide open, and I know I've made the right decision. As soon as we land, Sasha heads in another direction, and John and I head for home-sweet-home.

John has gone ahead with plans for a party on my actual birthday, despite my poo-pooing the idea. He amazes me with his event-planning skills. Typically, this is not where his talents shine. Seventy guests show up at this shindig in Macedonian Park — which is right around the corner from our home in Brooklin, just north of Whitby. These guests range in age from three to seventy-six. My husband puts together an affair to remember as friends and family swipe and swing a baseball bat with gusto at Barbie Doll pinatas, run three-legged races, play blindfold-croquet, and shoe toss. There is even a gold-fish race ... don't ask.

John has hired my African drumming teacher, Ron, to teach this birthday brood how to play an African djembe drum. Ron has hauled more than sixty drums to this event and the place is rocking with the bass resonance of these powerful instruments. Neighbours living across from the park come out to see what all the ruckus is about. It's magical watching my family and friends play the rhythm "I like peanut butter, I like jam" with glee until their hands are red-raw from slappin' the skin of the drum with gusto.

I rolled into bed that night vibrating from the effects of the day. I am so grateful to John for putting on a spectacular kids-of-all-ages birthday party for me. He hit it out of the park.

Chapter Two - BC Bound

My birthday bashing doesn't stop there. This is a birthday year that can't be limited in time and space. So, next up on the "best-birthday-ever" roster is time with my brother, Steve, in Salmon Arm, British Columbia (BC). The plan is to see as much of the Pacific Province as I can on the back of brother number two's Harley-Davidson.

In September 2008, I board the VIA train at the Oshawa station and settle in my seat prepping for the sixty-seven hour, five-province ride to Kamloops, BC. I chose the train route to give myself the gift of time. I want to rest and sleep, to be accountable to no one. How I wish this gift for everyone—space to think and embrace the quiet solitude with the option to socialize with fellow passengers or not, whatever calls you to do.

I vacillate between solitary and social time during my stay on board. I meet and greet people from all over the world walking the narrow hallways, sitting down for a meal, or sipping a cocktail up in the observation deck. Everyone I meet is in fine form sharing their "I'm froms" and their "going to's." When I am not being Chatty Cathy, I am hunkered down in my berth writing in my journal, meditating, reading, or snoozing. During daylight hours, there is a painted landscape of earthly delights to take in from every window of the train. As we chug through Ontario, my home province shows off her Canadian shield rock formations, farm-fields, and forests. I am amazed by how long it takes to plow through Ontario. It's larger than France and Spain combined. Did you know that? I didn't.

The train stops at Union Station in Winnipeg, Manitoba, for a spell; we are encouraged to visit The Forks Market, which is just a short jaunt away, to grab some food or souvenirs. It feels glorious to be out walking and breathing in the fresh air after being cooped up for so long.

We go at warped speed through Saskatchewan during the night to make up for the time we lost when making stops to take on more passengers. In the early hours, as the sun comes up, I'm cuddled up in my blankies in bed, peeking out the window and there before me is a brilliant slash of yellow whipping by. The wheat, canola, and mustard seed fields present like a Monet painting. This province really is as pretty as a picture.

Alberta's landscape is diverse. The prairie grassland, gentle rolling foothills, and badlands are surrounded and protected by the mountains. I am never bored seeing all that Western Canada has to offer from the train's vantage point.

I am starting to get excited as we are getting closer to my destination. I have no idea what to expect, but that's part of the go-with-the-flow headspace I am encouraging fifty-year-old Me to practice on this adventure.

The pièce de résistance is British Columbia. It's humbling, majestic, and wild. The Canadian Rockies are a natural wonder of this world and must be seen to be believed. I fight back tears at the magnificence of this country that I am privileged to live in, take in, and enjoy.

After three days on the VIA train, I arrive in Kamloops at twelve o'clock midnight. I depart the train and exit the station. There's my brother, Steve, with bear hugs that crush my tiny frame and a big, goofy sleepy grin. "Hey, Yo Yo. Good trip?" he asks.

"Fantastic. Loved it." I reply. "Thank you so much for picking me up at such an ungodly hour. I really appreciate it, Tee Tee." That's our family's nickname for him.

"Anything for my little sister," he says, which makes my heart melt.

Steven is the second oldest of my five brothers; we are four years apart. From an early age, this kid gave my parents a run for their money. Premature grey hairs sprang up, no doubt, due to his mischievous antics. According to our mom, if little Stevie didn't get his way, he'd throw himself on the floor and hold his breath until he turned blue; then, of course, Mom would cave.

If I were to write a song about this particular brother, I'd use the adjectives stubborn, defiant, tough, wild, and cool. Back in the day, a few of my girlfriends had a serious crush on him. The principal at Buchanan Park Public School would shudder when another Howard kid joined the new student roster. He knew what he was in for during the next six years because of the reputation of the first two little Howard hellions – Michael (the eldest) and Steven.

When I was five years old, I remember feeling lucky to have my big brother, Tee Tee, hold my hand as he walked me to baton lessons every Saturday morning.

Then again, he could be a real dick too. There was a pathway I took on the way to my school; it was lined on either side by a high wooden fence that was covered in people's names, initials, and who-loved-whoms, but mostly with naughty words. I was fascinated by these dirty sayings and took it upon myself one day when I was in Grade 3 to leave my own message on the fence with a piece of chalk I'd scoffed from home. I scribbled "Big Bum." I'd never done anything as scandalous as this before in my life.

Heading home at the end of that same day, my brother ran up to me and grabbed me by the arm. "You're in big trouble." Steve threatened to tell Mom what I'd done. Of course, I denied doing it. "Greg and I saw you do it so don't try and lie your way out of it." He had me and I knew he'd lord this stupid stunt over me for life. I pulled away from him and ran home crying terrified Mom would find out and punish me severely. I was petrified every time Steve gave me the stink eye after that if I didn't do what he said. I felt like the damsel, "Nell," being tied to the train tracks by the dastardly Snidely Whiplash in the Rocky and Bullwinkle cartoon show. Nightmares plagued me for weeks, which wore me down to finally confess—through a mess of snot and tears—to Mom about the bad thing I had done. Oh...sweet redemption. Funny thing, I can't recall what my punishment was.

Trouble seemed to follow me when I was with Steve. In the frigid cold of winter, we walked together one day to school, which was not a common occurrence. He usually walked to school with his hoodlum friends. He spied a snowplow on the school property and talked me into going for a closer look as the monster machine spewed out huge hunks of snow and ice.

"No, way, we're already gonna get heck. The bell rang a few minutes ago, so we're already late," I said, backing away, already feeling that panicky sensation running from my tummy, to my chest, to my throat. I was never late. I was six years old and knew punctuality was of utmost importance to teachers, parents, and other people in charge.

"We have to go, Tee Tee," I said, my bottom lip trembling.

"Who cares. This is more fun."

We turn our heads at the great roar and rumble coming from the snowplow heading our way. I scream and whip around to face my brother. My eyes give away the horror that I knew we were in for.

The massive chunks of ice and snow scooped up by the snow-plow from the ten-foot snowbanks and funneled through its long-necked blower pummel our backs, legs, bums, and heads pushing the air out from our lungs making it hard to breath. The blue wool winter suit and matching hat I was wearing did nothing to protect me from this brutal attack. I wailed in terror of being smashed to smithereens as Steve hoisted me up from my bottom and threw me over the red snow fence, pitching me face first into the snow, adding to the shock and pain of what had just happened. My brother looked for a spot where the snow lay high along the fence and vaulted over it with an "oomph" as he landed. We both stood up and watched the snow machine move along past us, totally oblivi-ous to what had just happened. "You okay?" Steve asked with a stupid grin on his face. I nodded, tears streaming down my frozen apple-red cheeks, wiping the ooze from my nose with my snow-clotted mittens, knitted by my Grandma Penhale.

He picked me up and carried me through the two-and-three-foot drifts into the school, wiping the tears and snow from my body, before dropping me off in front of my classroom. Hands atop her hip bones, my teacher, Mrs. Steele, gave me a stern look of disapproval for being late until she saw the state I was in. She walked me to the back of the class and removed my sodden snow suit and hung it to dry, then asked me to explain to her what happened, which I did through sobs and hiccups. I was ordered back to my desk and she announced to the class she was leaving the room for five minutes and expected us all to behave while she was gone. All eyes were on me when she left, and I bowed my head as a fresh wave of revulsion and shame washed over me.

Two minutes later the P.A. system interrupted everyone's thinking, with "Would Steven Howard please come to the principal's office?" It was repeated with emphasis.

The whole affair was big news by recess. I was told to go home with my brother, which felt daunting because now we had to face our parents. We were sore and bruised for a few days, but we were told we were very lucky that no serious injury had occurred, other than to our reputation. We made Buchanan Park Public School history on, "What not to do when confronting a snowplow."

This brother of mine left home at eighteen because he didn't like the rules under the roof, and he never looked back. In time, he became a biker bad-boy. Over the years, he had run-ins with neighbours, more principals, employers, the police, the judicial system, shopkeepers, and more smart alecks like himself because he liked to challenge the status quo.

I looked up to him, though, because he was a hard-ass, and took no guff from anyone. My first ride on a motorcycle had been on the back of Steve's Harley when I was fourteen and that I'll never forget—the wide-open space, the thrill, and the fear of going that fast with no protection, hanging on to Steve's mid-section with all my might. He was more at home on a bike than anywhere. Freedom is his calling and riding his Harley Davidson is one of his answers.

Like me, Steve was born in Hamilton, Ontario, but he moved to British Columbia when he was twenty-five and made a life for himself there. To everyone's surprise and delight, he married, Silvia, and had two girls, Jessica and Kimberly. We never thought he would marry, let alone have kids. Though now divorced some eight years from Silvia, his girlfriend, Colleen, lives only fifteen minutes down the road from my brother in her own English-garden country home. I know this because she sent me some glorious pictures of her handiwork. Colleen is the Martha Stewart of gardening.

Steve has always been a true-blue animal lover ever since horses snagged his heart at the tender age of ten. He even made his living working on the computer systems of several racetracks in North America so he could be near the horses. Today he is a gentleman farmer and landlord and makes his way back to Ontario once a year to visit his four brothers and little sister.

At the train station, Steve opens the passenger door of his Toyota Tundra pick-'em-up-truck and helps me get settled. It's an hour-and-a-half car ride to the city of Salmon Arm where he hangs his hat. Salmon Arm is situated along Shuswap Lake in BC's Okanagan Valley.

We pull into my brother's driveway, unload my luggage and head straight through the back door of his century home. Steve points out my bedroom and tells me where the bathroom facilities are. We are both bushed, so we say our goodnights, give each other a wee squeeze and head to our respective rooms for a good night's sleep.

After tea and toast in the morning, he wants to give me the "lay of the land," so I get out of my jammies and into some casual romping wear. His house sits on a one-hundred-acre parcel of land that has a river running through it and sits in a basin below Bastion Mountain. I am first introduced to the furry family that keeps my brother company so he doesn't get lonely living alone. There's Molly, a one-year-old black Bouvier, and Misty, the three-month-old Australian blue heeler, who is a voracious "nipper" of all things that move, especially the back of my ankles. She wouldn't let up, that little stinker, so I kept my distance from her. Steve thought it was cute; I wasn't amused.

I am not a lover of dogs; they make me uneasy. My dislike-affair with them began when I was ten years old. My brother, Phillip, who was twelve at the time, got himself a paper route. Our mom thought it would be a swell idea for me to help him. *Oh, great, just great.* In inclement weather, Mom would sometimes drive us over to our delivery route with the wagon jam-packed with all the papers and flyers which we covered with plastic garbage bags to protect them. It took a few pairs of hands to load it into the back of our station wagon. Usually, though, we walked the six blocks to get to our assigned route, wagon in tow, whining and complaining that the people inside the houses were sitting down to a hot dinner enjoying their warm, cozy abodes, while we were here pounding the pavement slinging grocery store flyers, papers, inserts, and sometimes "free samples" of new products. We were envious as hell.

Phil took immense pleasure in making me do some of the houses with the dogs, even though they weren't on the side of the street I was assigned to handle. There was one big, mean-spirited brute in particular who hid beneath a camper-trailer in the driveway of one of the houses. He looked like the dog on that popular television series, *The Littlest Hobo* but he had a Cujo personality, (Cujo was a vicious man-eating St. Bernard in the Steven King book of the same name.) I trembled as I tip-toed up the drive, making my way to the front stoop to insert the paper in the mailbox, hoping and praying "the nice little doggie" was inside his house, fast asleep. There was no law then to keep your dog leashed, so you were shit-out-of-luck (SOL) if they came at you. I hated this job with a vengeance. Some of our customers' canines would lunge and bark at me behind the closed front doors—or screens in the summer—and I'd practically jump out of the running shoes I was wearing; they scared the living daylights out of me. I even had a lady in the neighbourhood yell at me, shaming me for delivering papers on a Sunday. She said it was the Lord's Sabbath and it was sinful to be working on the day of rest. I was cast down, frightened, and embarrassed, and decided I would never deliver to her house again. I told my mother the story and she said she didn't blame this woman. "She had every right to reprimand you," Mom said. I was in the wrong, I guess, so obviously, I got no comfort or support. My Mother was a very moralistic church lady herself, and she too felt shame that her children got caught disobeying the fourth commandment. We never delivered on a Sunday again.

When owners who let their violent or volatile dogs run willy-nilly, I believe they should be paying for the therapy today for those of us traumatized by their psychotic animals. Come to think of it, I think my brother, Phil, should be paying for my "dog-trauma" treatment. Whenever I feel freaked out with fear or anxiety about anything, I refer to it as my "Facing the Dog."

In addition to Steve's dogs, Molly and Misty, he also has two horses, Pye and Ribby (who used to be racehorses), and several cats (I did not catch their names). Not only does he collect animals, but he is also a collector of all things "boy-toy"—vehicles, vintage trucks, Harleys, farm equipment, tractors, and every tool known to man.

After we say hello to his critters, we roam the land, and then he walks me down to the river and he gives me the low-down on the history of the area. I step a little closer to the water to see how deep it is, and both my feet sink deep into the drink. I didn't know where the water started or ended due to the high grass. My brand-new Merrell travel shoes are drenched. "Jeeeeez, Louise!" We march back to the house and I set the sodden footwear outside to dry on the back deck. Thankfully, I have my biker boots and flip-flops for backup. We spend the day just lounging and catching up.

The next day of our most excellent brother-sister vacation, we down some breakfast then layer-up to keep warm on the bike. Leathers are a must to cut the wind, which can be biting at times. I look rather fetching in my black boots, jacket and helmet, the head gear borrowed from Colleen, Steve's girl. I get Colleen to take a picture of Steve and his "Biker Mama-sister" to send to my husband, friends, and family. He tours me around all over who knows where and we stop at his customary "wings and beer" stop where they greet him by name. I order a salad for lunch, and he has his usual. As the first day on the road gears down, we drive up his driveway after a nine-hour toot around the neighbouring towns. I can barely get my leg over the bike to stand as my thighs are frozen open from having my legs spread sea-to-sea for so long. Nothing a hot bath, some Epsom salts and yoga can't cure, though. I do, however, walk like Hoss Cartwright for a few days.

It's day two of the Best of the West tour and I hook my fingers through Steve's belt loops aboard his 2006 Electra Glide Model hog

heading southwest of Salmon Arm. We weave and bob the highways, roads, and streets of Kelowna and area, past Big White, into
Rock Creek then make a stop for a tea, pee, and beer in Osoyoos.
Osoyoos is Arizona-dry/hot, like a desert. As soon as we arrive, we
remove our extra layers down to our T-shirts, otherwise we'd melt
like Frosty. It is a picturesque day and I'm wearing a perennial grin.
Back on the bike, I holler, "Penticton, here we come!" There's nothing like the feel of riding on a motorcycle. It's scary-fun, which is
just what a life coach would suggest for this halfway mark in my
life, I'm sure. The road is uncomfortably close when you look down,
and you hope and pray you never fall off, 'cause it wouldn't be
pretty, so I says to myself, I says, "Don't look down." I take in the
other drivers and passengers that are sharing our road-space and I
wave and smile. I suck in all the beauty I can from behind my
visored helmet: the brilliant blue sky, the artistic formation of the
clouds, the rocks, hills, and dales. You will never, ever, be bored on
the back of a bike. That's a promise. From lovely Penticton we blow
through Kelowna again on our way back to Salmon Arm for a well-
earned rest from touring.

   We take the next day off to hike the hills behind Steve's property.

Steve takes Molly, the Bouvier, and a shotgun with him for protection as there are black and brown bears up in them thar' hills. We sing tunes from the seventies to let them know we are here and mean "the Gentle Bens" no harm. My heart is racing, my eyes are wide like they're prepared to meet my maker, and my hands are saturated. I inform my brother this was not what I had in mind in order to get in a little cardio exercise. Yes, I am a born and bred city girl.

Colleen has us over for dinner and invites me to stay at her place for the next few days. Well, you don't have to ask me twice. We have so much to talk about and so much in common. We're both avid readers, have weird and wonderful physical ailments, we love to laugh and tease Steve, and we are both into metaphysics, nutrition, and self-development—we're a match made in heaven. We love the touchy-feely stuff. The next few days I am pampered up the wazoo with her culinary skills, both savoury and sweet. I languish in her backyard on a lounger surrounded by trees and flower gardens that would make the most famous gardeners drool. The following day, we drove into downtown Salmon Arm. Colleen shows me the library she works at, and we poke around a few of the city's boutique-style stores. I head back to Steve's the following day and after that, visiting some of my brother's friends is on the roster.

Vancouver, Victoria, Nanaimo, and Tofino await, as I had them on the gotta-see list, so my brother, Colleen, and I hop in Steve's big-ass truck and make our way to the Sunshine Coast. Seeing the majesty of those Rocky Mountains up close and personal lodges a golf-ball of emotion in my throat. It takes us just over five hours to get where we are headed.

Vancouver is the stunning gem of the Canadian West and is also known as Hollywood North because of all the movie filming they do there. Steve's daughter, Kimmy, lives here and works as an Early Childhood Education (ECE) teacher. Her place is about a twenty-minute walk from Stanley Park, which we plan to visit. This kid pedals her bike everywhere—to work, and shopping and social engagements, which is probably why you can bounce quarters off her thighs. This fun and wild-spirited kid is the apple of my eye. She adores style and vintage fashion, sports a new hair colour and look with each new season, and is a total non-conformist. She has one raunchy mouth on her, reads until her eyes bleed (just kidding, though she does read a lot), loves anything creative, and she is a little daredevil.

We knock on her apartment door and she answers wearing a boa constrictor around her neck. Today her hair is a rich teal colour, which looks glorious with the milky white complexion she inherited from her mother. We have a quick tour of her sweet, boho chic abode, then sit down for a drinky-poo and a quick catch-up. "How's life, how's work, how's your love life?" and all that crap. A half-hour in, we head out for dinner at a local Thai restaurant.

My friend, Lianne, who also lives in Vancouver, meets us for dinner; I haven't seen her for more than twenty years. I worked with Lianne at Maclean's Magazine back in the eighties. The air is blue with "literary talk" as Kimmy, Colleen, Lianne, and I are all addicted bibliophiles (AKA bookworms). Colleen has the inside scoop because she works at the Salmon Arm library, as I mentioned earlier, and gets all the new editions and reviews. Poor Steve can't get a word in edgewise. We feel bad for him, so we let him pay the bill.

Kimmy and I are both artists so the last time she came to visit me in Ontario—more than four years ago—I dared her to try something new and different with paint. "What do you have in mind, Aunt Yo Yo?"

"How do you feel about "booby" art?" I asked. Before I knew it, she had tugged her shirt off over her head, ripped off her bra, and said, "Let's do it!" That's my girl. I disrobed from the waist up and we glopped various paint colours over our breasts, grabbed a canvas each, and maneuvered our tah-tahs like paintbrushes to smoosh the paint around to create our masterpieces—"breastical bits" we called them. Boy, was that a gas and a half. No other kid of the twenty-three nieces and nephews that John and I share would I have suggested this screwball idea to, but Kimmy wears her "crazy" with pride, just like her Auntie Yo Yo.

After dinner we say our goodbyes to my friend, Lianne, and my niece, Kimmy. Our posse of three—Steve, Colleen and I—make our way to Victoria where we stay at the James Bay Hotel. It kinda feels like a girls' sleepover. We giggle half the night drinking rye and gingers reminiscing about the past and the silly antics of the Howard family, also known as the "Howeirds." Colleen has family members who own pubs in this city and they treat us like royalty. These pubs are not the little corner dives you see on television. These are first-class-designer poshy-pubs with solid carved wood and upholstered lounge chairs.

Next up, we do a quick tour of Nanaimo, then proceed to Cathedral Grove to see the mighty redwoods which give pause to the power and glory of Mother Earth. How small I feel in their presence; I embark on a major hug-fest with these towering giants.

From here, we hop on a ferry over to Tofino, which is a small district on Vancouver Island. Its wild natural scenery – lakes, inlets, and ancient rainforest—is a feast for the eyes. We spend some time whale-watching from dry land but didn't book an actual tour on this particular visit because I'd already had that thrill of a lifetime back in 1992.

Back then, my husband, John, my brother, Jeff, and I booked a whale-watching tour on a Zodiac boat with about ten other people and motored around Haro Straight, through the San Juan Islands and the Strait of Georgia, just off the coast of Vancouver. Captain Ron was at the helm searching for pods of Orcas in the vicinity. There were a number of other tours scouting for these beautiful creatures as well, but many reported no sightings after being out longer than anticipated. We waved goodbye to our disappointed friends as they headed back to land, but our Captain said he'd give the search another twenty minutes. Well, didn't we meet up with not one, but two pods of killer whales - grandparents, parents, and their babies. They came right up to the rubber dinghy and we could look them in the eye. Many were diving beneath our wee boat, which was kind of nerve racking, but we had no incidences of "man-overboard." The cast and crew on our boat were hooting and hollering and getting high on nature. The day was warm, sunny with a hint of mist on the water. It was one of those moments in my life that I felt a spiritual connection to these mammals, to nature and to God—more than I'd ever had. Tofino calls me to revisit it again one day.

Once home and settled from our road trip, Steve's ex-wife, Silvia, calls and invites me to join her and her girls, Jessica and Kimmy, at the Radium Hot Springs for a spa day, the day after next. *Uh, yah!* Kimmy is already headed our way via bus from Vancouver, and Jessica, the youngest, lives with her mom. Steve drives me up to Silvia's house which is a half-hour drive from his place. I spend the night at Silvia's and we girls watch "The Tudors," a drama series based on the early years of King Henry VIII's forty-year reign. It's brutal, bloody, intense, and erotic. We only watch two episodes, but I am hooked.

The four of us leave early the next morning for the spa, which is situated in the Village of Radium, nestled between the Canadian Rockies and Purcell Mountains in the East Kootenay region of BC. We are greeted by the smiling staff and invited to change into white, fluffy housecoats before being introduced to our personal estheticians. They lead each of us into separate rooms to enjoy the spa treatments Silvia had booked prior to our arrival. We all look baked and fried when we reconvene in the waiting area afterward. Reclined in white leather lounge chairs, we sip cucumber and lemon-infused spring water and doze, listening to the tinkling/ waterfall/ bird song music piped in from speakers overhead.

The hostess walks over to us fifteen minutes later and suggests we take advantage of the outdoor, naturally heated, mineral water pool; these hot springs are known for their healing properties. The spa's brochure explains that the minerals in the water help to heal the body by pulling toxins from it, which in turn strengthens the immune system. We soak our relaxed, sleepy bodies in what feels like a delicious hot bath, then diligently follow the prescribed protocol of slipping our warm, toasty bodies into the cold-water plunge pool, which is a rush to the system, let me tell you, but it is invigorating at the same time.

By the end of this glorious day, we feel all bright, shiny, and new as we drive back to Silvia's house. We four amigos are a little bewildered as to why the Radium Hot Springs and Spa markets themselves as a "spring" when it's just a couple of cement swimming pools. My initial vision was Silvia, me, Kimmy, and Jessica luxuriating in a hot-spring natural lake swimming around like mermaids, with a massive waterfall cascading down our backs as we stood beneath it. Wrong dream. We get a chuckle out of it because we never even thought to ask anyone at the spa the whys and wherefores of the name. Turning to more compelling convos about each of our experiences on the way home, my dear sweet sister-in-law apprises us that she treated us all to this day of relaxation and merriment, which was a very generous gesture.

"Happy Birthday, Yo Yo. Steve said this was a big one, so I wanted to spoil you. What did you end up doing for your big fiftieth, anyway? Wasn't your birthday back in June?" asked Silvia.

Chuckling, I share the "best birthday ever" plans I'd concocted earlier that year to celebrate not only my big day, but the whole year of merriment. I tell the girls *some* of the details of Bimini, the party John threw for me, the crazy idea of a sexy dance party with all my besties, and this wonderful month in BC. Oh. Sexy dance party? Well, a few weeks after my birthday party, I'd hired a burlesque dancer who arrived at my house decked out in black stockings, garters, heels that gave her a six-inch vertical lift, a merry widow, and a pink feather boa. The basement served as our dance stage and she gave me and my friends instructions in the art of burlesque. The moves we performed looked more like Stripping 101 because, surprise, surprise, some of my friends are a little dramatic, and hambones to boot. The instructor began by teaching us how to pull off a long glove with our teeth while making Marilyn Munroe-moony eyes. The next trick was to flick and flap our colourful feather boas and hyper-gyrate our hips as the ten of us channelled our inner Gypsy Rose Lee with luscious abandon. We had a ball, and we were absolutely exhausted from laughing and moving so ardently. I absolutely love my dearest friends' enthusiasm for supporting the sweetly warped part of me.

After our spa day, I spend the night at Silvia's and we resume our Netflix obsession with that bad boy, Henry VIII. My sister-in-law drives me back to my brother's place the following day. Even though she and my brother are no longer together, she is still family and I adore her. Steve is still good friends with her as well, which is nice.

Steve and I spend a few more days tooting around on the bike, but time is creeping up as the month of September rolls to a close and it's time to head back to Ontario. My brother and Colleen offer to drive me to Calgary, Alberta, where I can pick up the train in Edmonton, which gives me a chance to see more of what Alberta has to offer, and to meet Colleen's grown children.

We bunk at Colleen's daughter's house in Calgary for a few days and take in the sights of the city. On the final day, I catch the Grey-hound bus up to Edmonton, which will connect me with the east-bound 3:00 p.m. VIA Rail train home.

I join the throng of passengers waiting outside on the platform of the VIA station. We crane our necks as we anxiously watch and wait for the oncoming train. An hour drags by in a hotbed of raised voices and tempers wondering where the hell it is.

Finally, a voice blasts over the Public Announcement system informing us tired and hungry travellers that there is a delay in the train's arrival due to an accident on the same rails a few towns away, and the wait could be a while. The VIA staff invite us to go to dinner at nearby restaurants where our meals are compliments of the company. After that they will have more information to share with us. Bonus! I get a free dinner and some time to hang out and chat with many wonderful people from all over Hell's half acre.

It turns out it's a nine-hour delay in departure which, frankly, just adds to this salute to "Yay-I-made-it-to-fifty, and "shit hap-pens" kinda feelin'. In the end, because of the delay, I am awarded a free VIA Rail pass which affords me two round trips for two – one to Ottawa and one to Montreal, which we take advantage of the following year.

It's well after midnight when the train finally pulls into the Edmonton station and the thirty of us exhausted, not-so-happy-now campers climb aboard. It's bed-time-quiet as the passengers who have boarded in Vancouver (and the thereafter-stations) are now all tucked in for the night and down for the count in lah-lah land. The Porter on the train points our weary group to our respec-tive berths or passenger seats and we scatter like cockroaches. It appears I have three other bunk mates in my sleeping car by the sound of the snores and heavy breathing coming from behind the drawn curtains.

All I can think of is sleep, a solid bed to lie in, and maybe a cup of chamomile tea; the tea will have to wait. I haul my suitcase up on the bed, unzip it, and grab my jammies, toothbrush, and toothpaste. I'm too stinking tired to wash my face, but I have to brush the fur from my teeth.

I yank off my shoes—you know, the new Merrell's I wore only once before they got a soaker in the river the very first day of my stay at my brothers? I silently gag, hoping my dinner will stay where it belongs. "Sweet Jesus," I whisper. In hindsight, I really should have soaked my shoes in sudsy water with a bit of bleach to kill any bacteria before I left them to dry because the god-awful stench, which would make a pig-farmer wince, is permeating the entire rail car.

I am frantic the disgusting odour will awaken the other passengers from their blissful sleep because of the confined space. I have souvenirs in my luggage wrapped in plastic bags, so I grab one of the bags, dump the gift I bought for John into my carry-on, then throw the offensive footwear in, double knot it, then toss the bag back in my suitcase. I haul my biker boots out at the same time and place them on the floor for me to wear in the morning.

I'm like a drunken sailor, bouncing off the walls, as I make my way towards the bathroom, which is the size of a broom closet. I haul one leg up into the tiny stainless-steel sink, hang on to the edge of it with the other hand to avoid toppling over, and turn on the hot water faucet. In the early hours of the morning the train travels at breakneck speed. It takes a sharp corner on the tracks and I fall ass over teakettle, my legs flailing in the air, and hit my head on the back of the bathroom door. I rub the back of my noodle as I right my wrong position, and resume washing the stink off my feet. Thank goodness there is a soap dispenser on the wall, as my bar of Dove is in the toiletry bag in my suitcase. First foot done, I heave the left leg up into the sink and suds up the left foot, while still hanging on to the sink with all I've got.

My eyelids are at half-mast as I crawl in between the crisp white sheets. I'm bone-weary but wired; my body is shivering. I pull the curtain to my berth closed. I don't remember anything until I'm jolted awake by commotion all around me. The neighbours I heard snoring in the night are up and at 'em early, likely heading for the dining car for breakfast. I peek out the window as I see the sun has joined us. I roll over and surrender to the calling of "more sleep, please."

The remainder of the trip is sweet and solemn as I spend most of the time in self-induced solitary confinement. Best gift to myself ever!

John is at the station to pick me up after this last hurrah in the birthday bash lineup as it comes to a close.

I am pleased as punch with myself for honouring this lifetime milestone and making it one I'll never forget. I set out to challenge myself, learn, grow, face my fears and, indeed, I scaled this mountain. If you don't challenge yourself or do something that is out of your comfort zone, more often than not, life will find a way to do it for you. You are the only person who can give you what you really need and desire. It truly is an inside job. This is usually not about external stuff, but more about listening to your heart and what it longs for first and foremost; the rest will follow. My heart and soul yearned for adventure, fun, connection, play, and me-time. I got everything I wished for. Plus, I believe I racked up three birthday cakes.

Life is like being on the back of that motorcycle. Even if it scares you because you feel unsteady or you feel like you might fall off, hang on, but not too tight; you want to enjoy the ride. It's all about enjoying the moment, right then and there, and then going forward into the wind (future) while being open to receiving the miracles life has to offer. Just like that train being late to pick me up in Edmonton, it could have been a complete shit-show, but that one little hiccup came laden with an armful of gifts ... wonderful conversations with strangers, a free dinner, snacks, alone time, and two free trips for two on VIA.

"Aging is not for sissies," Academy Award-winning actor Bette

Davis once said. I give myself a hardy pat on the back for the dedicated effort I put in toward making this year one for the books. I felt more vibrant and alive with each new experience I planned and executed. My fiftieth was a celebration of how far I'd come in my life, the high roads and the low roads, while giving me oodles of time to evaluate the precious present and what the future could potentially hold. The possibilities were endless.

Too Cool at the Pool

I met a guy at the community swimming pool the other day; it's situated three doors down from our condo in Florida. Initially he was standing watching the wildlife hang out on the man-made pond the size of a football field that lies just beyond the deck of the pool, and he had his back to me. Not wanting to disturb his reverie, I closed the gate quietly, placed my gear on a deck chair, climbed down the stairs and slipped into the temperate pool water. I then began my dogpaddle/breaststroke, double-combo signature move gliding from shallow to deep end.

He made an about-face and our eyes met and I got a simple nod. The ever-so-shy me stood up in the shallow end and said, "Good morning."

"Hey," he offered.

"Hope I'm not disturbing you."

"No, ma'am.

"Do you live here?" I asked, referring to the River Strand golf community we, my husband and I, live in."

He shook his head, "Hawaii."

Huh, didn't see that one coming, I thought.

"What brings you to Bradenton?" I asked.

"Having a place built in Parrish," he said, nodding his head in a northwesterly direction, "about a half hour from here. I'm renting here in River Strand temporarily. Plan to be here six months and Hawaii the other six."

"Sucks to be you, eh?" I teased.

He smiled.

"You must love the heat, too. I'm from Canada. We had one of the worst winters ever this year.

With a smirk, he said, "Ya, I picked up on the "eh."

This manly man with the aviator glasses and USAF cap was

guarded, cool, and clipped. Handsome bugger, too—over six feet tall, ramrod straight, and well built. He had kind of a Tom Cruise look on a Tom Selleck body. He wore freshly pressed slacks and a crisp white, long-sleeved shirt open at the collar. The only casual-wear were the Dockers on his bare feet. My good sense taps me on the shoulder and hints, *maybe he wants to be left alone.*

"You a military man?" I ask.

"Just retired."

"Oh, where did you work?"

"The military."

"Ah," I replied.

Just then my husband, John, arrived with beach towel and book in hand. I brought him up to speed on the conversation thus far with my new poolside pal. John dove right in and shared with the man that he, too, was a new retiree. As I tootled in the pool with my noodle, the boys discussed the pros and cons of living in a gated community.

The gentleman shared that he'd bought some acreage in Parrish. "So, I wouldn't have neighbours looking in my windows on either side of me. I want privacy so I can ..."

I finished with, "walk outside naked and pick up your news-paper?"

He snorted and nodded. We all had a chuckle.

"You're not afraid of break-ins where you're going to live?" I asked.

"If someone wants to get in, they'll get in; these are the times we live in. Everything is replaceable, right?"

Burglaries along the west coast of Florida were becoming all too commonplace, whether you were in a neighbourhood with security or not.

I asked him about family—grown kids, a couple of grandchil-dren. I didn't get a warm and fuzzy Grampa-vibe from him. Much to my single neighbour, Sue's, chagrin, I forgot to ask about a Mrs., but this guy wasn't forthcoming with this juicy detail. My hubby steered the conversation back to work. "What part of the military did you serve in?"

"Special Ops."

Holy Hell, I felt like we'd just bounced from a Danielle Steel novel to a Tom Clancy.

It begged to be asked, so, I course, I did. "Did you serve over-seas?"

"Afghanistan, Iran, Africa."

That explains the strong, silent type. No doubt everyone and his brother wanted to pump him for dirt and details. Television and the News were no substitute for the real deal.

"Must have been pretty scary over there in the Middle East." John said.

"Some," Mr. Military Man replied. "Never been afraid of dying though. Worst fear is going out slow and messy—a quick bullet to the head is the preferable exit of choice."

Silence ensued while we all took a visual snapshot of his comment.

"Case in point, I have a quick story I can share." he offered.

John and I were all ears, like kids around a campfire waiting for the ghost stories.

"Back when I was twelve years old, I was in a car accident with my folks. I died. Saw the tunnel, the light, the whole shebang. He sighed and said, "An immense sense of peace came over me I'd never felt in my life and I haven't since." He went on to tell us there were two young men who appeared before him on "the other side" who said they were his brothers.

"That's not true. I'm an only child," he countered.

These young men told him it wasn't his time to die; he had to go back because his life wasn't over yet and he still had things to live for.

This mystifying man explained that when he recovered from surgery, clearly recalling what had transpired in the great beyond, he shared his near-death experience (NDE) with his mother, hoping for some clarity and comfort from her. She burst out crying and ran out of her son's hospital room. Weeks later he found out from her that she'd had two stillborn babies before he, her third son, was born.

"Wow," my husband and I said in unison.

"Since that time, the thought of death doesn't bother me," he continued. "The military was an obvious and easy career choice for me."

I counter-shared the beautiful synchronicity of our meeting that day as I was currently reading a book called, *Dying To Be Me* written by Anita Moorjani. At age two, she and her family moved to Hong Kong. Her memoir describes the discontent and struggle they had in living with cultural conformity in this country, while being of Indian descent. The high level of constant stress, she believed, led to her getting cancer in her forties. She was wasting away at barely seventy pounds. Her husband wanted to ease her pain by taking her off life support, but her parents, being Muslim, didn't believe in "pulling the plug." They believed the day of your death was God's decision. Anita slipped into a coma and was transported to another realm. The author's delicious description of her esoteric NDE tempts you to take the trip to "the wild blue yonder" earlier rather than later. On the other side, she was given the choice to either stay or go.

With an expanded awareness of who she was and where she'd been, she chose to return to her mortal body. After that it took her a few short weeks to heal from the disease that had ravaged her body.

It was our new friend's turn to be 'wowed', and he thanked me for the book recommendation, then gave me one of his own. He suggested I read, *Life After Life* by Dr. Raymond Moody, a book he keeps well stocked in his office for people he meets suffering from shock, grief, and adversity. This Dr. Moody was well known for his studies and documentation of several patients' NDEs forty years ago.

We tied up our three-way by saying, "Isn't it strange that nobody showed up to use the pool this entire time?" We said our goodbyes, good lucks, and good talkin' to yas. We never saw this cool dude again.

Live and Loin

I'm a frazzled gal, I'm feeling stuck,
I work crazy hours to make big bucks.
I'm kissing fifty and losing steam,
My "to do" list'd make the Buddha scream.

Indigestion, headaches, insomnia, and pain,
Light a fire under my ass, there goes my GO Train.
Run here, run there, and "don't forget the bread,"
If I go any faster, I swear I'll be dead.

It's the job, the kids, that mole on my back,
A frantic commute aboard the fast-track.
That bloody carrot dangles before my eyes,
Tempting me to believe it's cruel lies.

I'm high, then low in this crazy rat race,
The stress is stamped all over my face.
My foundation is wobbly, not very sound,
Probably wiser to seek higher ground.

The good girl in me says, "I'm fine, it's all good."
I'd give anything for peace—no, really, I would."
What the hell am I doing? I'm trapped like a rat,
When will I be happy? Huh? When exactly is that?

It's kinda funny when it comes to brass tacks,
The ego's M.O. is to defend and attack.
Who said I was damaged, I'm never enough?
Me, that's who; now I call its bluff.

Life's a reflection, a metaphor, you see,
Of the stories we create, both you and me.
Play with it all, there's no way it's wrong,
That's the polarity talking, just singin' its song.

I've got trillions of cells who've got my back,
They're quick on the ball when I'm on the wrong track.
It's my job to listen, give thanks and praise,
For their incredible service, and the symptoms they raise.

Here's a cool thing I do to get outta my head,'
I do the opposite of what my small self just said.
If something I do makes me tense and uptight,
I turn it around until it feels right.

When I'm quiet and still, anxiety lowers a notch.
If my mind starts to blather, I just witness and watch.
I surrender and breathe down into my toes,
Dropping into that state where wisdom flows.

We're beautiful humans, brilliant, divine,
With a skill set our Higher Self's working to refine.
Hey, we're not broken, of that I am sure,
God sees us as perfect, innocent, and pure.

I'm giving up the ruse, who I think I should be,
I'm a child of the Universe; yep, li'l ol' me.
I'm a piece of the puzzle of Heaven on Earth,
It's time I wake up to my own self-worth.

Strange Bedfellows

My friend, Carolyn, introduced us. The attraction was purely physical and instantaneous. She's as natural as they come and her smell? Earthy, organic, clean.

She's the giver and I'm the taker in this relationship. She's dedicated to servicing me at all hours; skin-to-skin, she pleases me.

I take her everywhere I go, if it's appropriate, that is.

She's easily manipulated, malleable even, though tough on the outside and soft and gushy on the inside.

I have to admit, she's not my one and only. She herself gets around but I don't mind. As a matter of fact, I often initiate introductions to others extolling her warm, sweet endowments. I've even caught her in the arms of my husband on occasion.

She's not perfect, by any means. She has her hot spots and can go from one extreme to another. But I warn you, don't get too close or she'll burn you ... even leave a mark.

I'd love for you to meet her. You'll warm up to her instantly. Everyone does. Know why?

'Cause she's my *heat bag!*

The Story of Life

1st Decade—It's all about Me, Me, Me!

2nd Decade—It's about people liking Me.

3rd Decade—It's about, "Hey, look at Me."

4th Decade—It's about, 'Hey, what about Me?'

5th Decade—It's about me understanding and loving Me.

6th Decade—It's about "I gotta be Me!"

7th Decade—It's about saying NO to others and YES to Me.

8th Decade—It's about "mirror, mirror on the wall, what the heck's happened to Me?"

9th Decade—It's all about ME! ME! ME!

10th Decade—It's about "Hope to Hell there's still a Me.

Let's Face It

I'm going to shrink-wrap the 2019 year I had in a tidy little "hell-ya" bundle.

It began with an all-expense paid trip for two to Cuba, compliments of my dear friend, Melanie, who won the prize through Trip Central. She answered their three trivia questions every day for twelve years, and they called her up in October 2018 with the news her name had been chosen.

"I want you to come with me," Melanie said.

That's a double hell-yah!

I arrived home lightly toasted at the end of February after lolly-gagging on Cayo Coco beach for a week with my dear friend. I unpacked, did laundry, then packed up the Toyota Highlander as John and I were heading to our southern abode in Bradenton, Florida for the months of March and April. We left there at the end of April and tacked on a week in Hilton Head, SC to break up the drive back to Canada, and to dip our toes into the Atlantic.

In June, I flew across the pond to Germany and England with my dear friends, Lizzy, Anita, and Eva. The trip's highlights were: Sidney Crosby, the hockey player, was staying at our hotel and spa (we got pictures with him to prove it), I hiked a mountain in the Alps, and Anita and I ogled two young German men in their birth-day suits showering in the spa facilities. I warned the guys there were a couple of uptight, inhibited ladies from Canada passing through and they might want to cover up. Their reply? "Don't vury ladeez, vee are not shy here in Cherm-un-ee" and then they waved us through to the steam room, chuckling away.

The hot, humid summer gave way to the cooler nights and shorter days of autumn as my husband and I and our friends, Kerry and Sandy, saw Spain and Portugal via Insight Bus Tours for three weeks in September. We did a whole loop-de-loop starting in

Madrid, then popping down into Portugal, and from there made our way to Seville, Cadiz, and Gibraltar, home of the big rock. Our last stop was Barcelona whose prized possession, the Sagrada Familia, is a sight to behold; it literally takes your breath away. The building of this church began in 1882 and soon hit Basilica status as it grew and grew over the decades. Today, in 2024, it is still unfinished as they keep adding more steeples. One of the highlights on this trip was the home-cooked meal put on by the local women in a small town in Portugal. There were forty of us on this bus trip and four generous women each welcomed and fed a group of ten from the group. Though we couldn't speak each other's language, communing around the table and eating brought us together. Both of these countries and their people were an absolute delight, and a must on the European list of places to see and experience.

In mid-October, one of my besties, Lizzy, and I drove south to Florida, with a quick stopover in Asheville, NC for an over-nighter with our friend, Jennifer. Lizzy and I slept in a cozy camper in the backyard – all we were missing was the bonfire and marshmallows. Since it was close by, we managed a quick visit to the Biltmore Castle, an 8,000-acre estate built in 1889 and thereafter owned by George Vanderbilt, the son of Cornelius Vanderbilt, in the Blue Ridge Mountains of North Carolina. It was an icon during the Jazz Age. This two-hundred-and-fifty-room French Renaissance chateau opened to the public in 1930. Judy Garland, Bing Crosby, Al Capone, and President Roosevelt all stayed in this breathtaking mansion.

Lizzy stayed with me at our condo in Florida for two weeks, then headed home. John arrived via air a few days later and we stayed until mid-December, flying home for Christmas.

The year 2019 was a treasure trove of travel and adventure. I'm so glad I had these memories deposited in my happy bank, because what was to come was going to drain the joy-juice from my account.

My sixty-two-by-four (to the head) 2020 year was a rip-roarin' cluster-fuck.

Oh, it started out with swell intentions—in mid-February a dream-come-true was realized for my husband, John, who was about to turn sixty-five. Disney World, Universal Studios, and particularly the new Wizarding World of Harry Potter roller coaster ride were at the top of his wish-list of things to see and do for this milestone birthday. From there, we planned to head to our condo in Bradenton, Florida, again.

I opted out of the Harry-ride (as mentioned previously, I am prone to vertigo) and waited patiently for him outside the entrance to the popular attraction. The poor guy staggered out the exit door the colour of green pea soup. We drove one and a half hours in complete silence after he'd whispered to me, "Can we please not talk. Focusing on the road is helping me not hurl."

After a few days of settling in, buying food, and cleaning our sweet sanctuary in the south, my muscles and joints began to ache and throb. My energy decided to go for a long winter's nap and I slept for the better part of the next two weeks. I suspected I had the Disney-flu from that petri dish of cooties, courtesy of the little people in the magical land of make-believe.

John and I are not big TV news watchers, but our families and friends liked to fill us in on current local and world events. "This Just In" stories were spreading about a deadly virus said to have come out of Wuhan, China. This COVID-19 virus was causing some serious health concerns, even death, in the East. It put the entire nation in pandemic-panic mode. We were all worried about what this could mean for ourselves, our loved ones, and the world, but one of the saddest and most disappointing consequences was the "every man for himself" mentality. So much for the evolution of our species. The hoarding of water, toilet paper, and groceries was, frankly, insane, and it all flew off the shelves in grocery stores, gas stations, and hardware stores like people were prepping for the Apocalypse. Stockpiling became commonplace followed by the "uglies"— vaxers versus anti-vaxers, Trump trashers versus tooters, world-wide, shameful finger-pointing about whose beliefs and opinions were right or wrong between countries, spouses, families, neighbours, and friends. Neither my generation, nor those follow-ing, had ever seen nor experienced anything like it. In my mind it had the makings of the Spanish Inquisition,

The nation was inhaling the perfume of some mighty fine, toxic shit. My faith in mankind was sorely hurting.

We stuck it out in Florida until the end of March 2020. Our families and friends urged us to return home as there was talk of military intervention and border closures between the United States and Canada. We left March 26th and decided to drive the twenty-three-hour trek straight through to Hamilton, Ontario, "Do Not Pass Go, Do Not Collect Two Hundred Dollars" à la Monopoly, stopping only for tea, a pee, and a fill-up. I'd packed enough food to eat on the way to last this road trip all the way to Alaska. The highways were almost barren and we were the only ones at the Border Customs when we went through. It was kinda spooky.

Once home in Ancaster, everyone was ordered by the government to stay inside and see no one, save those living at your own address. Groceries were ordered on-line and picked up outside the supermarket, or one poor sucker from the family was elected to brave it in the store, replete with mask, sanitizers, and a somewhat strong constitution. Compulsive hand washing, the cleaning of produce, and disinfectant-drenched surfaces both in and outside the home became the new norm during the COVID CRAZIES. Masks were mandatory throughout the land.

I surmise when this generation dies, of those who survived this worldwide event, they won't need to be embalmed with formaldehyde, should they decide to be buried. This planetary COVID crowd will be pickled quite handsomely with the chemicals from all the hand sanitizers and anti-bacterial wipes we religiously doused on our bodies during this tumultuous time.

Typical of the human condition, some were pessimists and complained, others were optimists and hoped this pandemic would soon be over, while the realists took one day at a time and adjusted their sails. The carefree, however, sat back, read a book, played with their kids, made love to their partner, went for long walks, and watched the boob-tube.

John and I did our best to stay away from the "fake or otherwise" news and commenced micro-dosing on daily outdoor exercise, comfort foods, board games, and uplifting reading material. We spent many hours cyber-connecting with friends and family on

Zoom. We overindulged in the Netflix/Prime department—we became insatiable gluttons, really, bordering on addiction. Our favourite movies and series were *The Kominsky Method*, *The Crown*, *Upload*, *The Queen's Gambit*, *The Big Little Farm*, *Younger*, and *Marco Polo*, to name a few.

I nursed and soothed my hyper-wired nervous system through holotropic breathwork, meditation, journaling, writing, and painting. John became a die-hard puzzle-monger. There was a whole lotta fear and anger risin' to the top that had been nicely buried within each and every one of us, and if anyone tells you differently, they're frickin' liars. Our tendency is to cram that terror, hurt, and trauma right back down in the dirty sewers of shame and blame where it was originally packed in tight, simmering on the back burner until a catastrophe of epic proportions came our way and unhinged the pressure cooker valve. It didn't take much to set any-body off during this time.

2020 was a wakey-wakey call for all of mankind. The bright shiny ray of light in the dark cloud of fear and uncertainty were the gifts this pandemic presented - kids miraculously began playing outside again, families ate healthy home-cooked meals and played games together around the kitchen table. Zoom was a number one hit nationwide which brought our global family together in both business and play. Many worked from their home offices and home-schooled their kids. Generally, there was less: pressure to go/do/be/have, VISA expenses, gasoline charges, car mileage, vacations, shopping (other than online,) and the good old-fashioned cold/flu. And terrorism? What terrorism?

People threw down money for online masterclasses, podcasts, videos, Ted-Talks, and YouTube subscriptions which opened up computer-accessed continuing education like never before. The media world was hungry to sell the lonely, sick, anxious, broken-hearted, and the insanely bored all the answers to their prayers. People were desperate to do something, anything, hence, the resur-gence of gardening, painting/writing classes, and do-it-yourself projects. Even though Value Village and Thrift Stores were closed, many dove into decluttering both their closets and their minds, dumping all the shit they no longer needed. What we all discovered was we could live with less crap in our life, literally and figuratively. This new less-harried life was like a soothing balm to our fried and frazzled nerves.

Laundry was on the "load-down" as many stayed in their pajamas or comfy clothes all day because there was little to do and no one to see outside the walls of home. Flour, sugar, and butter disappeared in a wink off the grocery shelves as many blew the dust off Grandma's recipes or googled meal plans and started cooking up a storm.

John and I were adjusting to being together 24/7. As luck would have it, we'd arrived home from Florida earlier than expected so we threw ourselves into the spring project we'd planned, building a sunroom onto the back of our 1950's bungalow. Architects, framers, electricians, roofers, city planners, and the reams of building sup-plies to order and pick-up kept us busy for the spring and summer months. In mid-June, I noticed a small nodule the size of a small chickpea on the side of my right cheek (the one on my face.)

No biggy, looks like a sebaceous cyst, I thought. I waited a bit hoping it would go away. It didn't. I called my doctor's office and they set up an on-line appointment—doctors were only seeing patients for emergencies during this heightened pandemic scare. The Doctor agreed it looked like a harmless cyst, as far as she could tell over the computer screen but she asked me to come into the office for a closer look.

Dr. G. decided to refer me to a dermatologist to get a second opinion. It took a few weeks to get in to see the skin doctor, but when I arrived, she saw a hint of a shadow behind the pesky protu-berance that raised some concern (and my anxiety), and she decided to take a biopsy of the affected area.

Two weeks later, I was informed that the lesion was a squamous cell carcinoma ... yup, cancer. It was a "holy fuckerballs" moment. From the time I noticed the spot on my face to the diagnosis six weeks had passed and the growth was growing. My next step was to get in to see a Head-Neck-Surgeon.

Oh, yippee.

Turned out Dr. C., my ear-nose-and-throat (ENT) guy, was a pretty good egg and I put my trust in him fully—as if I had a choice. We couldn't book my surgery until the biopsy results came from the Dermatologist, but they went AWOL. Dr. C., my head/neck hero, was furious and decided, finally, to order another biopsy of his own, which of course, took a few more weeks to get results.

Oy!

This virulent COVID-19 virus was certainly not helping my situation in the least. But wait, no, actually, it did. Masking-up was my saving grace. When most were whining and complaining about having to wear a mask, I was grateful for the fact that I could cover my face to hide the nastiness I was experiencing, at least to the outside world. I rejoiced in being able to go for walks, shop in a grocery store, and visit friends and family without the questioning glances at my facial carbunkle. The health department was easing up on restrictions by now.

The summer months proved to be both riveting and revolting. Watching the 16'x 28' sunroom going from plan to completion was thrilling and kept my spirits buoyed.

While John worked tirelessly on our building project, I entertained myself with CAT Scans, MRIs, PET Scans, radiologists, oncologists, biopsies, colonoscopy, endoscopy, naturopaths, functional medicine doctors, lab visits and of course, I can't leave out the eleven COVID-19 tests necessary to enter the various medical facilities. All visits were made solo as no one was allowed in with me to appointments. My dear husband drove me to every one of these, using the waiting time to run up and down the steps of the escarpment, which were close to the hospital. After my appointments, we'd go for a walk to lighten the heaviness. John swore he'd never felt better in his life from all the cardio he was doing.

In a month and a half, the tumour was growing aggressively now—it was about two inches in diameter, and it had weird red veining around it. However, this did not speed up the booking process as all non-emergency surgeries had been put on the back burner in the medical hot spots. COVID-19 patients were taking precedence. The longer the wait to get this thing removed, the more potent the cortisol chemical bath splashing my entrails in an already compromised nervous system became. Yup, I was a wreck.

Because of the size and severity of the growth and its proximity to my right eye, I was sent to an ophthalmologist. The doctor couldn't have been sweeter, and I am so grateful for her calming demeanor. She would be assisting the head/neck surgeon in the operating room to remove the cancer, which meant I would be having eye surgery, as well.

I hit stores to pick out flooring, windows, doors, and other building supplies to get out of the house and keep my mind off my troubles. During these chaotic times, you had to book personal appointments to get into these places.

To keep myself further occupied, I enrolled in writing classes, walked daily, practised yoga, fed the troops who were building the sunroom, co-created an online writing group, "Tea-Time Tales," and watched myriad painting and health-related videos.

Finally, on October 22, 2020, I had the tumour removed at St. Joseph's Hospital in Hamilton. Recovery was a bitch. My naturopath gave me the best prescription to healing she could: "Lois, this a perfect opportunity to fully embrace loving yourself, no matter what."

After five days in the hospital, I stood in front of the mirror in the bathroom adjacent to my hospital room as the nurse peeled off the bandages. Witnessing the damage, my knees buckled, just like you read in the books. I felt woozy and had to sit down.

"Are you ok, honey?" asked the nurse.

"Uh-huh," I nodded but inside I'm screaming, *Of course I'm not fucking okay!* The face that looked back at me in the mirror would make Vincent Price wince. The right side of my face had been sliced, diced and Picasso'd. The head/neck surgeon had cut and peeled away a large triangle of skin from the right eye, cheek, ear, and neck to remove the carcinoma. Thankfully, they got it all.

The silver lining of my convalescence was I got to languish on our couch in our bright, shiny new sunroom. Even though it was now November, the temperature in my "recovery palace" got north-ward of twenty-five degrees Celsius due to the in-floor heating and wall-to-wall windows. If you don't know me well, let me just say I am a hot-lovin' woman, temperature and otherwise.

My friend, Lizzy, lent me the entire series of her Louise Penny book collection, thirteen in total at the time, which kept me occupied between naps. Louise is a brilliant, hilarious Canadian writer who lives just outside of Montreal. Getting through them was slow and steady as I only had one good eye to read with, which tired easily from the strain.

Between John and my friend, Val, (my friend since Grade 7), they helped me wash my greasy, matted hair and change the dressings, which was no easy feat. God bless their pointed little heads. I was instructed to, "by no means get the bandages wet," so we had to come up with some inventive ways to avoid facial drench. I want it to go on record that those hospital shows on television do not reflect the truth of what you look like post-surgery. My vanity sashayed in, noted the "new look" and bellowed like an injured bull moose.

When adversity comes a-knockin', so do the ones who have your back. Food, flowers, gifts, phone calls, emails, and texts came in by the droves. Even a four-foot purple octopus (helium balloon) arrived on my doorstep from our friends Kerry and Sandy, which tickled me pink. Oh my God, it made me laugh. Best gift ever, though the prepared foods our friends and neighbours dropped off were pretty awesome too.

I didn't realize how attached I was to my face until I was forced to endure a new design, not of my making. This challenge was totally "in my face" and one I couldn't hide from the world. My health-account was draining and I felt raw, humbled, scared, and vulnerable. I have had some pretty intense surgeries in the past and already lived with strange neurological symptoms, vertigo, digestive issues, and chronic pain so this latest challenge kicked me square in the chops.

The next step in this continuing saga was thirty rounds of radiation.

From November '20 into January '22, came another onslaught of doctor's appointments, blood work and tests. To prep for the radiation, one medical crew member unravelled what looked like a fist-sized wad of cheesecloth over the entirety of my face and neck.

"I got this. I'm okay," I soothed myself with comforting thoughts. Then I wasn't.

The netting material began to harden and squeeze my facial muscles like the walls were closing in. A hyper-alert, "Run for the Hills!" electric zing coursed from my toes to my nose. A frantic need to "am-scray" took hold of me, but I couldn't get up. I took deep breaths down into my diaphragm to keep the claustrophobic-crazies from turning into a full-blown panic attack. A half-hour takes her sweet damn time, and they finally remove the dreaded helmet of Hell and instruct me to call the office the next day to receive my appointed radiation dates.

Psyching up for these treatments took some mighty fine work. My ol' friends, fear, anguish, and anxiety, were sent to the canvas on a creative deep dive. I slammed, smeared, and whipped the worst of the worst words I could think of ... fuck, hell, asshole, bitch, motherfucker, cocksucker, bastard, and shit in vibrant magenta, orange, Bimini blue, raging red, and lemon-lime green with a giant paintbrush and had my way with them on canvas. I poured out my rage and frustration by going bigger, bolder, and stronger. It was cathartic to scream and release these emotions out of the simmering cauldron of my mind. The gift from my guts was a sobbing release of pain and tension, which had been neatly folded, pressed, and tucked into the bottom of the hide-and-protect-at-all-costs drawer deep down inside me.

Months later, my brother, Darren, came to visit and was nosing around my art studio and came upon my hissy-fit art piece. All I got from him were some raised eyebrows and a curious grin.

Day One of the thirty rounds of radiation took place in mid-January 2022. I was instructed to climb up onto the table and lay on my back. The top of it was cold as a tomb and hard as concrete; no padding to cushion the blow. I'd lost thirteen pounds from all the stress and reclining supine felt like bone-on-bone agony. A young radiation therapist walked into the radiation room carrying the space-agey-looking mask that held the outline of my face. It was trippy seeing my face outline in this creative form. He began placing the contraption over my face and said, "I'm going to lock the cage into place now." I pushed his hands away from my face and bolted up to a sitting position. "Oh no you don't," I said with less force than what I felt inside. He was shocked and looked over to the radiation technologist for help.

I asked, "Did you take Psych 101 as part of your training?"

"Um, yeah," he replied slowly, no doubt wondering where this was going.

"Please, never refer to this thing as a 'cage' again," pointing to the mask. "Nobody wants to feel like they're being caged in, okay?"

He stood there mutely, once again glancing to his colleague for back-up, no doubt summing me up as a crackpot. From across the room, the radiation technologist's eyes moved from his to mine. She smiled and nodded, and I knew I had an ally.

"Can you refer to this contraption as my 'crown' from now on, please?" With obvious reluctance, he nodded his assent and brought the "crown" down over my face and shoulders. To add to my comfort and joy, in order to remain dead-still for the radiation beam, he bolted and locked the mask into the table so I couldn't move. Breathwork, I need you, STAT! I prayed forty years of yoga would not fail me now.

I'd placed Gelsemium tablets under my tongue to ease the anxiety prior to the procedure, but this homeopathic remedy wasn't potent enough to quell my nerves. As much as I abhor unnecessary pharmaceutical drugs, I ordered a prescription of Lorazepam from my GP PDQ to get me through this ordeal.

Can I tell you these sessions got any easier? Nope. After five rounds of radiation, I developed an angry—big surprise—red, pus-filled, fuck-me, two-inch boil in the middle of my back right along the spine. It was agonizing to lie on that tortuous tabletop with the pain pulsing and radiating. My GP insisted I leave it alone and not touch it. I cried in my husband's arms one night, and after throwing around some ideas, we devised a plan to cut a hole in a maxi pad (I kept them on hand for guests) to cradle the angry abscess from the hard surface of the table. That didn't work either. Fed up and furious, John insisted on lancing the sucker himself, and OMG what a relief. I'd have gagged squeezing out all that foustaciousness from this sucker but bless his strength and determination in helping this boil go away and it did.

Throughout the entire thirty rounds, the radiation team got in on the "royalty" game and everyone referred to the mask as my "crown" when I arrived daily. The day I rang the bell to signal the end of my treatment many of them gathered to clap and cheer me on and Jane, the radiation therapist I saw the most said, "Lois, your reign here is now over." I felt like bawling.

The radiation experience opened my eyes to how virulent this disease is and how it doesn't discriminate. I met people of all ages and all walks of life who were going through the same cancer circus-act. It's hard to write the word "cancer" as it evokes a pickle jar of mixed emotions ready to spill ... the sweet, sour, tangy, tart of them all. This uncomfortable word is everywhere these days— television, books, magazines, social media, newspapers, and billboards, and it shows up in myriad conversations. It's there to remind me of the lurking boogeyman ready to jump out and pounce at any time. I practice surrender to the inward torment of these thoughts and send love and compassion to those parts of me that are kicking and screaming at the injustice of it all.

Post-radiation, I was burnt out, literally and figuratively. The mucous membranes of my nasal passages were fried like pork rinds, and I looked like the poster child for the annual Rosacea Conference. My poor tongue was so toasted, it felt like kitty-cat-tongue-medium-density sandpaper. I have always been a bit pale and pasty, especially in the winter, but now sported rosy cheeks and a somewhat gimpy smile due to nerve damage. After the surgery, my right eye drooped like a basset hound's and leaked runaway tears. My nose dribbled snot and blood like they were in a hurry, and I blew through Kleenex tissue like an overworked psychiatrist. Once again, I thank COVID-19 for the gift of masking to hide my facial sorrows.

Because my nose was plugged with dried, bloody scabs, I was unable to breathe normally. After forty years of putting up with my husband's snoring, the tables turned, and I was now causing a ruckus with my open mouth and plugged pipes, waking him three or four times during the night.

I vowed I would never take tasting, smelling, breathing, whis-tling, kissing, singing, eating, or yawning for granted ever again.

In December of 2022, I was booked for a follow-up plastic sur-gery for a "clean up on aisle four". The ophthalmologist fixed my eye as best she could, but my mascara days were over, sadly, as I no longer have lower lashes on the damaged peeper.

The young, dark-haired, bespectacled doctor who was to perform the plastic surgery on my face reminded me of Clark Kent, and I shared this with my friend, Melanie.

"Who better to do the work on you than Superman, honey," she'd replied. We both thought this was hilarious.

I repeated this story to another friend, Kim, and her response was, "Not only that, but Clark Kent operating on his beloved, Lois. How perfect is that?" I just adore my brilliant friends.

It's been over three years since the cancer was removed from my face. My little self still has those underlying fears of, "What if it comes back? Could it show up elsewhere in my body? Is it my time to die? I'm not safe. What if?" These are thoughts that make me human, I suppose.

What can I say I have learned from this ordeal? Well, for start-ers, I've learned I can't attach myself to anything in this life for too long, anyway, because "everything is impermanent," according to the doctrines of Buddhism. Life is all about change and there's noth-ing we can do about that. However, we do have control of how we see, react to, and interpret what is showing up on a daily basis. Is it easy? Nope. It takes a whole lotta practice. But maintaining a healthy, accepting, and loving mindset is what will get us to the finish line with few regrets and a full heart.

When fear, anger, frustration, and anxiety come a-callin', I let them rant and rave and have their say without pushing them away. This is a work in progress, of course, and again, I must practice this every day. A recent example is that I was booked for a CAT Scan, an MRI, and a follow-up appointment with the head/neck surgeon. I have to go every six months for five years after I had the cancer removed from my face. Because of the past trauma with all the shocks I've had with several diagnoses over the years, going through these tests are akin to me being boiled alive. Okay, I may be exaggerating—I've been known to do that—but it brings up a tsunami of overwhelm so that I don't sleep for days prior to diagnostic tests or seeing a doctor. My body has been wired for some time to think, "something bad's going to happen or something is wrong with me." This is referred to as "being in survival."

Today, regulating my nervous system is just as important as flossing and brushing my teeth. Breath work, body scanning, humming, singing, exercise, getting out of my head (fearful thoughts) and into my body is what keeps me from experiencing what is referred to as the sympathetic state (flight, fight, freeze), instead of the parasympathetic state (rest and digest). I allow myself to feel and listen to the voices of fear, agitation, frustration and anger and let them be there without wishing them away, or pushing them back down from where they came from, or resisting them. "What you resist, persists," they say. These thoughts and beliefs at one point in my past protected and served me, but accepting and understanding them today is what helps when I go off into "freak-my-freak" mode. They need to be soothed and know they are safe.

The society in which we live, especially the one I grew up in, teaches us to squash, censor and suppress our heavy feelings, but we all know you can run but you can't hide. We spend our lives chasing, wanting, demanding, wishing, and yearning for the "if onlys" which is exhausting. We forget the beauty and gifts in this moment, and the next, and the next. I am mindful to take joy in the little things that make my heart sing every day. Gratitude is at the top of my to-do list for all the beautiful people I have in my life that make me laugh, and who care about me. Before I go to bed, I begin taking deep breaths to calm and centre myself, then I recall the best of the best of the day, celebrate and give thanks for whatever comes to mind. This is like my own personal peace project, a ritual extending love and praise for my life, however it is showing up. By doing this, I believe I am doing my small part in making this world a more loving and harmonious one.

Arrival Gate

Based on a visualization meditation symbolizing my true essence and brilliant potentiality.

I float upon the wondrous depths of nothingness. A speck I am, a mere mote of matter amid the tranquil sea of Presence. I am a brilliant ray of light emerging from a mother who reaches evermore to embrace her seekers.

I ride particle and wave with my friends. We touch, bounce and bind, then separate to go our own way to explore new places. Amidst the movement of our distinctive dance is the infinite quiet. It's there … look for it. Here is the joy, the gift you've been searching for.

I gaze toward the Giver of Life and a smile wakes up my heart's face. Home, my origin of breath. I'm coming...wait for me.

Shits and Giggles

It's been a rip-roarin', bitchin' nightmare of a time in my life of late. And I'm not even going to apologize for my language as my mother has passed through the pearly gates, so I won't get hell from her for my potty mouth.

I sat in the Radiation Department's waiting room passing time on my cell phone wondering when they were going to call my name. I'm here for number twenty-five of my thirty rounds to blast the affected area where I'd had a squamous cell carcinoma—a cancerous tumour—removed from my right cheek.

I spark up a conversation with the couple sitting across from me. They had to drive in from Port Colborne, which is well over an hour's drive from Hamilton. The husband is a big, beefy guy with a curious accent, who obviously adores his food and beer. Okay, I'm just assuming here. His wife, by the sound of it, is from around these parts. Mr. sits back in his chair, rests his head on the wall and lets the wifey do the yap-yapping, as we women so naturally excel at. A few minutes later, I ask her man if he is Aussie or Kiwi.

"New Zealand," he replies. He reminds me of some poor bugger headed to the gallows. I inquire into his story of what brought him to the Juravinski Hospital.

"Cancer," he spits out.

"Today is his first radiation treatment," the wife kicks in, no doubt to make up for her husband's harsh retort.

"Ah," I smile in sympathy.

I want to wrap my arms around this big galoot like cooling aloe gel on his burning rage, but these are COVID-19 times and I can only soothe with my words.

His wife explains that her husband is recovering from surgery for a tumour and has several weeks of radiation and chemo looming before him. His eyes speak volumes, but he still gets off showing me

146

his five-inch, twenty-two stitch incision on his fuzzy noggin' that would put Harry Potter's scar to shame.

I tell him and his wife my own sweet tale of woe when they inquire, and end with, "It's been the worst of times, it's been the best of times."

Mr. Kiwi smiles at my poetic joke and with an upward chin tug, and a curious smile, seems to ask me to elaborate.

"Well, my relationship with my husband has grown bolder and stronger in this shit storm, for one. This is the time when you have to face the scary conversations and possibilities set before you."

The couple face each other with loving eyes and nod.

"You also discover the friends and family who are with you during life's thicks and thins, and the ones that aren't have to be discarded and thrown in the recycle bin. I never felt so much love and support during my darkest days.

Again, simultaneous nods.

"Hanging out at a cancer hospital makes you face how temporary and impermanent our lives are, and how we take them for granted until a crisis comes a-callin'. Hearing other patients' stories has left me feeling humble and thankful. A few I spoke to were living on borrowed time."

"Lois," Jane, the radiation therapist calls from across the hallway. I stand from my chair and gather my coat and purse.

I look at the husband and assure him, "These radiation sessions go faster than you think. Trust me. I only have five appointments left of thirty, but I felt exactly like you do now. Wonderful meeting you both, and good luck."

"You as well," the Mrs. sends back.

"Thanks," her husband replies, our eyes connect in commiseration.

I wave goodbye and follow Jane to the "deep fryer," thankful to be ticking another treatment off my list. I lay supine on the table and take deep breaths as I feel the tentacles of panic raise their freak in my already hyper-wired think-bowl. The mask contraption is placed over my head to avoid any movement while the radiation beam bakes my unfriendly cells.

This isn't my first rodeo, so I sing songs in my head or recite all the people in my life I love and what I love about them. When I'm done that, I find myself ruminating.

"Shit happens while wearing this skin bag. It's inevitable. Just like the crap you deposit in the white porcelain bowl every day. You face it, examine it, then flush it away, and ta-dah ... you get a fresh start, a doo-doo over, if you will. Life is never always dark and dirty, just a series of shits and giggles."

Remember Who You Are

The idea for this story began with the thought, "If I were to write a fairy tale to myself as a child, what would I want to say to Little Lo Lo? Based on the adage,"if I knew then what I know now," what sage advice would I give that sweet, innocent, little dumplin'?

Mya heaved up a silent scream inside her head the likes of which she'd never felt before, and the rest of her body parts joined in with relish. Her low back throbbed, her hands were shredded and raw, and her once dewy skin now looked like a scalded, plucked chicken thanks to the searing rays of the sun.

She was lying on a smelly, old, straw mattress—no doubt slept on by someone from the last century—with her cousin, Roberta, by her side. Their room was upstairs in the attic of the ancient farm-house, far and away from any warmth and comfort from the fire-place on the main floor. Roberta grumbled under her breath, mourning the featherbed she'd given up. She glanced over at Mya and quietly said, "Yer fun and games are over fer ya now, Missy. Life is defferent here, not what yer yoosta." The two girls stifled their giggles at Roberta's new-found vocabulary, a gift they could thank the influence of the family they were temporarily living with for having bestowed. The girls kept their voices down as they'd often hear puzzling, offensive sounds come from beyond the thin walls of the house. Roberta then rolled over, bid her "good night," pulling the sheets off Mya's chilled body, and began her ritual snorfling and snuffling as she settled into deep slumber. Checking that her friend was out cold, Mya reached beneath her pillow—which had never seen soap, water, nor fresh air in its lifetime—and retrieved the gift her mother had given her upon departing for this "grand adventure",

149

or what Mya had thought was going to be an "experience she'd never forget." She sad-laughed at her naïve trust in those who were supposed to love her the most. Mya caressed the smooth stone with the number eight carved in it. She tried to recall what the eight signified—Love, Compassion, Honesty, Integrity. She stopped there. The first four of these life principles that her mother had passed along to her had already been broken by her parents. She felt cheated and betrayed by them. Kindness, Enthusiasm, Courage, and Patience were the next four principles that arose from her memory; she felt she could do a much better job practising these ones herself, especially with the loathsome way she'd been acting of late. She swiped at the hot tears that rolled down her icy cheeks. Salty sadness turned into a mess of sobs and she forced her face into the foul-smelling feather pillow to set free the unfettered misery she felt.

Mya's parents had told their daughter of their plan to go abroad for an extended period due to national obligations. They also informed her they were sending her out into the world to "see how the other people live." Her mother told Mya it would be an "experience she would never forget." Her cousin, Roberta, was to join her for the duration of the stay to keep her company.

Mya remembered the glorious day she and her cousin had left home, not knowing where they were headed. They both chattered like magpies at the prospect of their new-found freedom. Roberta, who was two years younger than Mya, had assisted her up into the crude, dilapidated rig, lifting the hem of her prickly homespun dress as she did so. Roberta then hauled herself onto the hard wooden seat across from her best friend. They were both clothed in simple brown frocks to hide their position and status. Mya's father explained that their identity had to be protected, which explained the horse, carriage, and clothes. The driver hya'd the horse onward. With one last wave to the family, they lurched toward the new horizon that lay before them. It was an arduous journey along dirt roads pockmarked with potholes and rocks. Mya had taken this time to practise talking the way she'd heard the villagers talk on the rare occasions her father had taken her on trips to survey his land and its people. It went against everything her tutor had taught her, but she enjoyed the crude way the words sounded in her ears.

It was a shock when Mya and Roberta realized they had been billeted at a pig farm, complete with a farmer, his wife, and their eight children. *For a period of one year!*

The family had been previously told that the two girls required lodging for a time as Mya's mother was hospitalized due to a weak heart, unable to care for her husband, nine children, and niece, Roberta, whose mother had died five years earlier. The farmer was handsomely compensated for the girls' room and board—paid for by an outside source, hired by Mya's father, to keep his identity unknown.

Mya and Roberta had been reduced to hard labour, well beneath their station, and after barely a month, Mya was beyond exhausted. The farmer and his wife expected them to feed the repugnant slop to the pigs and cows, clean out the chicken coop and horse stalls, rake, hoe, harvest, and pull weeds in both the family vegetable garden and the surrounding fields. In addition to their outside duties, they helped with the day-in and day-out meal preparation and kitchen clean-up—*who knew how much was involved in making food for just one family?* The housekeeping, as well as the care of the two younger children, was also part of their twelve-hour work days.

Still wide-awake staring up at the attic ceiling, Mya recalled feeling outraged at not being invited along on her parents' extended voyage. They rarely left her at home when they travelled. *I hate them; I do. How could they do this to me?* The pain at her temples felt like a sledgehammer pounding away at the walls of her brain, and she had to unclench her fists and jaw to help herself relax. Then came the guilt, thinking she'd done something wrong and was being pun-ished, though nothing she had done came to mind. Her mother's, "An experience you'll never forget," forged a mocking promise in her mind. *What if I can never go home?*

Mya's personality began to change as did her circumstances. She succumbed to her farm-life fate often filthy, homesick, and furious. She was exposed to mice, mould, bone-chilling cold in the winter, and stifling heat in the summer. When nature called there was no attendant to whisk away the chamber pot; she was forced to go outside to do her business in the field, then bury her waste. She was reduced to finding leaves for wiping as clean rags were a luxurious thing of the past.

The farmer and his wife treated their boarders no differently than they did their own unruly brood. The Missus bellowed, swatted, and cursed them all to maintain order and upkeep in her limited domain.

The rage and frustration that infected Mya's very being was taken out on the innocents ... the animals, and the two little ones, Emma and Alice. Mya even pinched them on the back of their chubby little arms just to make them cry, which gave her a hint of sick satisfaction. Her fury was also unleashed on the older children in the family when they taunted and teased her and Roberta for the way they spoke. She felt herself unravelling as she punched, slapped, screamed and spit in retaliation. She'd never done anything like this in her life, nor even witnessed this unseemly behaviour, which just added to her guilt further.

Mya's thoughts continued to plague her as she lay wide awake thinking, thinking, thinking. She'd noticed these past few months she no longer skipped and sang as she had done since the time she had been a little girl. Singing was snuffed out the first week she'd arrived at the pig farm—"no singin' tolerated here, Miss Head-In-The-Clouds. Dere's work to be done." Rest was for the wicked, according to the Missus.

Trips to the surrounding villages were reserved for picking up farm supplies, selling fruits and vegetables, or lending a helping hand to neighbours in need. Both Mya and Roberta had been picked to go on a one-time visit to the town nearest the homestead, but all Mya had witnessed was more hardship, dust, dirt, and toil. Finally exhausting herself, her mind decided to call it a night, and off to sleep she went.

Princess Mya had grown up in a world devoted to her every want and whim. At the age of thirteen, King Edwin and Queen Matilda had decided it was time for their only heir to experience life outside the castle walls for a period of one year. She would live among the commoners, accompanied by her cousin, Roberta. Roberta's father, Prince Robert, was King Edwin's younger brother. Mya and Roberta's identity was to be kept secret and known only to those the king and queen trusted.

Mya's dreams of being free of the cloistered rigidity of castle-living for the first time kept her awake at night. Visions of adventure and intrigue had her counting the days until she would leave on her adventure, and her parents never let her think otherwise. After much strategic planning, the day of Mya and Roberta's departure finally arrived. Lifting her daughter's right hand, palm up, Queen Matilda placed a small burlap-wrapped gift in it.

"This talisman is to remind you of your true nature, my dearest. The number eight marked on this stone reflects the principles of life for you to follow—Love, Compassion, Honesty, Integrity, Kindness, Enthusiasm, Courage, and Patience. Practice these and they shall guide you through the most formidable times. You've only caught a glimpse within your short life of the wonderous world you come from. Life outside the castle will challenge you, Mya, and it may be hard to recall your former life. Fear not, for this stone holds great power and wisdom, and will always protect you now and forever-more." Mya gave a tremulous smile of gratitude, having no idea what her mother was trying to impart to her, but she clutched the gift to her heart anyway, sensing its future worth.

Allowing for the teary farewell of his wife and daughter, King Edwin pressed the details of the journey, as well as a purple velvet drawstring bag full of gold pieces, onto the steadfast driver of the ancient carriage—borrowed from one of the servant's relatives. The king drew the ear of the bedraggled old horse down to eye level and whispered to him with a sense of conviction and purpose. The horse nodded its head. Mya bit her bottom lip to keep the tears at bay as her father then took his turn giving his daughter a quick embrace and lots of encouragement.

Upon awakening the next morning, Mya's head felt lighter and less burdened, feeling more at peace. Roberta had obviously let her sleep a little longer, as her side of the bed was cool to the touch. She dressed, made the bed, and headed downstairs, making her way outside to do her business. Once done, she washed up with the rain water from the massive barrel by the farmhouse, and entered the kitchen ready to start the breakfast routine. Roberta sent a quick smile her way. "Sit yerself down, Miss Sleepyhead. The kids have eaten and 'er doing der chores. Your friend here said ya had an unsettled night, don't cha' know, so I thought ya could miss making da porridge just 'dis once. We left ya some eggs and sausage, haven't we, eh?" said the Missus. Her dear friend brought the covered plate to the table and placed it in front of Mya. "Dig in," Roberta finger-coaxed her. Mya felt truly special and thought maybe, just maybe, her luck was changing.

"Hurry it up, der girlie; we got work ta do dat won't get done by itself with the two of ya jabberwallin' all the dang day," the Missus said sternly, ending the command with a slight smirk on her lips.

"Moira," the heavy-set, weather-beaten farmer bellowed to his plump, pinch-faced wife from the front yard. Opening the front door, The Missus returned, "Whetcher' screamin' at me fer, husband?"

"Send de girlie," he nodded in Mya's direction, "straight away to Widow Brown's place. I be needin' some of dat salve that she makes fer de horse's shins."

A light sparked in Mya's eyes as she dutifully threw back her breakfast, then recited the directions to the widow's place back to the farmer's wife. Roberta crossed her arms, huffed, and stomped out the back door, feeling thoroughly insulted she had not been included in the errand.

"And no dilly-dallyin'. Give dis bread to Mrs. Brown, she's all but skin and bones dese days, poor ting. If you're not home by dark, de wolves will getcha and you'll be of no use to no one, hear?" the Missus instructed.

Mya took off like a jack rabbit through the pastures, first the farmer's, then the neighbour's, then down into the gullies, finally slowing to catch her breath. She came upon a beautiful meadow with long, green swaying grasses settled around an immense pond ripe with new sights and sounds. The sun's rays caused the water's surface to sparkle as though it were full of gems. Mya's heart burst with joy at this unexpected sight and ran to the water's edge. She peeled off her heavy stockings and plunked her feet into its delicious depths. In and out she dappled her toes, wiggling off the caked-on dirt that had accumulated since her last bath. She was aware of the sun baking the top of her head and she closed her eyes as she inhaled the perfume of the vegetation. Even the birdsong invited her to stay.

"Thank you I will," she relayed to the feathered ones above. "Can't stay long though, I have to pick up the medicine," Mya muttered to herself.

"What's medicine?" a voice called out behind her.

"Who's there?" Mya demanded, lurching to a standing position. She looked around and saw nothing but trees, water, and lush foliage.

"Is somebody there?" she repeated in a quivery voice. She heard a rustle and swung around.

A porcupine ambled towards her, calm as you please. Mya had never seen the likes of this odd creature, but had been versed by her tutor in many animal species.

Mya took two steps back.

"Do not be frightened, m'Lady. Peter Porcupine at your service," he said with a gentlemanly nod.

"You can talk? How do you know who I am?" Mya asked, her mouth agog.

"Indeed, I can converse. And we know many things about you, Princess."

"Who's we?"

"Why, we who live in the forest, of course. Come out and meet

Princess Mya, everyone." The elderly porcupine waved his friends to join them. From the bushes, trees, and underground warrens came deer, rabbits, squirrels, birds, raccoons, an owl, frogs, a dragonfly, bear, and skunk. Mya clapped her hands in delight. "Do you all have the ability to talk like me?"

Smiles and nods answered her question.

She felt somewhat wary of how these creatures knew so much about her and her face betrayed her thoughts.

The deer stepped forward with her two fawns and bowed her head; her little ones followed suit.

"Your Highness, do not distress yourself. Your parents requested we watch over you during your one-year sojourn away from the castle. We have been honouring this promise and relaying messages as to your progress.

Mya's eyes welled up at the mention of her beloved parents. *Who knew my parents could talk with animals?*

"We know how unhappy you have been these past months, Princess. Your mother sent us a message to pass along to you," the Owl explained.

Sniffling, Mya stared deep into the depths of the Owl's orbs.

"Don't forget the talisman she gave you and the message it came with ... Remember Who You Are, Princess," the owl reminded her.

Everything went quiet; the silence was deafening. Mya's eyes burned, and she tried to hold her grief and homesickness in, but it could not be contained and out it burst. "But what does that mean?" she screamed, which rattled her insides and made her anger roil.

"That's all they had to say in all the time since I've been gone? How could they abandon me, and to a pig farm, no less?" she screeched.

"Her Highneth thaid you would underthtand the methage," the skunk squeaked out, his body trembling.

The Bear stood on his hind legs and declared, "Me thinks all who hold a beating heart are worthy of all good things, especially friendship. We're all the same, but not the same. Do you remember the eight principles of life your mother recited to you when you first began your journey, Princess? They are Love, Compassion, Honesty,

Integrity, Kindness, Enthusiasm, Courage and Patience. Making them a part of your life is all part of 'Remembering Who You Are.' My friends and I, standing here before you, practise these virtues daily."

Mya remained dazed and confused.

The Porcupine took up residence beside Mya and instructed her to sit. "Princess, nothing in life is as it seems," Peter Porcupine began. "See these quills?" He pointed out the obvious. "Nobody would come near me for fear of being speared. Feeling frightened for my life is my only motivation to strike, but no one understands this. I never had any friends until I met up with these fine folks. I learned many years ago you can let life beat you down or you can make the best of what's been given to you."

"I want to go home; I miss my parents." Maya wailed, releasing the woes long held inside. She poured out the truth of being tormented, teased, and humiliated by the older boys at the farm and ignored by the girls.

"They all hate me! Rory, Egan, and that snot-nosed Bryan threw worms at me." After catching her breath, the Princess exclaimed, "Dora, Maisy, and Rosie call me and my cousin uppity and odd."

Pity and guilt consumed her, because she really did have a soft spot for the two younger bairns, Emma and Alice, but was fed up with being responsible for them. When she had exhausted the waterworks, the animals gathered around her to give comfort.

"Your time here is precious and on purpose," a raven said from a nearby branch. "Be an example for this family you live with; show them life doesn't have to be a struggle. We can all choose to think differently in our heads, even if the circumstances never change. If you want something different, you must think differently." All the animals nodded.

"Remembering who we are is up to each one of us. Nature doesn't have to learn this, we are born knowing this. So are you, but you forgot—most humans do. Your Highness, remember you are loved by the great beyond, and you hold the power and strength of it within you. It is guiding you in every moment, and it is protecting you always. You are magical, brilliant, perfect, and worthy in every way."

"Your parents chose to have you live among their people for a reason—to teach them the power they hold in their hands to lead happier, more productive lives. The king and queen are responsible for a portion of this, but not all of it. The rest lies within everyone individually," the squirrel added. "We all have this gift."

Mya whimpered, "I thought they did it to punish me."

One of the frogs croaked, "Your Royalness. You cannot teach what you do not know. You have to apply this wisdom to your own life first."

A light went on in Mya's head. She remembered the burlap-wrapped rock her mother had given her which she'd tucked beneath her pillow. "I think I understand now. Thank you so much for helping me see differently. I'm feeling better now."

The dragonfly landed on her Ladyship's shoulder and whispered in her ear. "Let your thoughts float by like waves on the pond. When the mind is quiet, we can speak to you and guide you through your life. The secret is to ask for our help, Mya."

Just as she was about to ask the dragonfly another question, the flying messenger was gone. She stood up and thanked all her new-found friends. Her heart felt lighter than it had in a very long time.

One of the raccoons looked to the sun and declared, "You must be off, Miss. It's getting on and you have somewhere to be."

Mya reluctantly waved goodbye to the woodland creatures as they themselves all headed home. She skipped and sang all the way to Widow Brown's, who in fact, was delighted to have the young girl's company. The kind woman offered up strong black tea and bannock with currants, and invited her to come visit again.

Ointment in hand, she raced all the way back to the farm and presented the wrapped package of medicine to the farmer.

"That's a good lass. How's the widow faring? She yammer yer ears off?" the farmer asked.

"No sir. She was very kind to me. She even offered me tea and refreshments."

"Oh, 'refreshments' is it now, Miss High and Mighty?" Get yerself inta' da' hoose and help da' Missus wit da' supper. Off 'ya go now," he said, patting the top of her head, which caused a deep warmth to course through Mya like heavy syrup.

Roberta ran up to Mya as she entered the farmhouse through the kitchen door, her beaming face and open arms conveying to Mya that she had been missed. Mya then ran up the back stairs to the attic. She lifted up the filthy old pillow and retrieved the rock her mother had given her. She tucked it into her skirt pocket and vowed to carry it with her forever.

Over the following months, Mya practised making the best of her circumstances and embracing the life principles her mother had passed along to her. She hummed while doling out the slop to the filthy pigs and other animals. The dreaded weeds became a game of yanking out old grudges and hurts. Housework was fulfilling now because she decided it felt good to help the overburdened farmer's wife. The Missus, she knew, was grateful for the help she and Roberta provided.

Even the eight varmints felt a change in their parents' tempers, and they all became noticeably calmer and easier to live with. They secretly hoped Mya and Roberta would stay longer, as eventually, their time began nearing its end. Besides, when the chores were divvied up amongst them, it made for lighter work for each of them.

Departure day arrived and the two young ladies reluctantly said goodbye to their surrogate family, although they were anxious to be on their way. The ride home was long and uncomfortable, which made dozing tricky.

Mya fell into her parents' waiting arms once the girls and their bags were unloaded from the rickety carriage.

"Mama, Papa, you're back! How was your trip? I want to hear all about it. Oh, it's so good to be home. I was angry at you both at first, but now I'm glad you sent me away; I learned so much," Mya gushed out, finally running out of breath.

"All in good time, my dear child. You can tell us all about it at dinner this evening. A feast has been prepared in your honour. And Roberta's too, of course." Mya's father's eyes twinkled.

Revelling in the copper tub's hot, sudsy water in preparation for the evening's festivities, Mya closed her eyes and focused on quieting her mind. She watched her thoughts swim by like waves on water. She summoned her new friends of the forest from deep within.

"I'm home, dear ones. Thank you for your help along the way," she whispered to them.

"You're most welcome, Princess," came a collective response from the quiet abyss in her mind.

"Now, don't forget ...," they said.

"I know, I know ... Remember who I am."

Queen Mya took her rightful place on the throne ten years later at the tender age of twenty-four, after her father succumbed to an ailing heart. Her mother, Queen Matilda, thus began to fulfill her promise to pass along the wisdom, magic, and healing arts that she herself had learned from her Aunt Elizabeth, many years ago.

Back then, the responsibility of Queen Matilda's training had been passed to her aunt, as Matilda's mother had died an early death at the age of twenty-one from influenza. In desperation, her mother's oldest sister, Elizabeth, or Lizzy for short, was summoned. This was highly unorthodox as her aunt was considered a pagan, making her an outcast despite her royal lineage. Lizzy had been adamantly against being any man's property and defied the conventional pursuits of the female gender — needlepoint, letter writing, and awaiting a suitable man's proposal. At the age of eighteen, she left her childhood home and her highborn life behind to seek freedom, independence, and higher knowledge. This left Matilda with little family and she spent most of her time with Nanny, her tutor, and the servants. Her father soothed his broken heart at the loss of his dear wife, Mary, with cards, drink, and women.

Matilda's Aunt Lizzy had a wild, coppery mane of curls and green eyes akin to a feline's. She lived a free-spirited life in a modest dwelling within the forest and she communed with the trees, plants and animals. She was considered a deity amongst most villagers, but was also feared by a suspicious many both in the castle and in the outlying villages. It was rumoured she could read people's thoughts, their physical afflictions, and the future. Healing was her gift and she devoted her life to using herbal remedies and magic to cure the maladies of the people within the confines of the kingdom and beyond. She was also the busiest midwife in the land, and hers was the first face many children saw as they were pulled from their mother's warm bellies upon entering the cold, cruel world.

Two weeks' prior, Matilda had been told by the royal physician, after a thorough history and medical examination, that she would never sire an heir due to scarring from a childhood infection which had rendered her barren. She'd only been married to King Edwin for one year. The news of her unfruitfulness sent her to her bed with a deep melancholy that nothing and no one could remedy.

Upon entering Queen Matilda's rooms, after a rather chilly reception from the palace staff, Aunt Lizzy asked the ladies-in-waiting to kindly leave the room. She perched on the side of her niece's bed, placed a warm, dry hand on Matilda's forehead, and gazed into her eyes. Her niece, she realized, looked more like her than her dearly departed sister, Mary—God rest her soul.

"Am I dreaming you, Aunt Lizzy?" Matilda's eyes fluttered open. She had not been allowed to see her aunt for a very long time as wary eyes and ears within the castle believed Elizabeth was a sorceress and would likely put a hex on them. Sitting up from her sick bed, she embraced her aunt with all her might, as the anguish of her barren condition ripped through her.

"I feel your sorrow and heartache, dear one, but I have had a vision. Cry no more, for I have glad tidings. You shall bear a girl child in the fourth decade of your life, and she shall rule the kingdom for many years—well after you, the King, and I are gone. She will be endowed with many gifts—goodness, strength, and a purity of heart that will keep peace throughout the land as long as she reigns." The young queen began blubbering once again until the welcome gush of relief dried her tears.

"Your life, Matilda, is about to change far more than you ever dreamed, for it is every woman's destiny to awaken to her personal powers by accessing the sacred energies of this world and beyond. These special gifts are bestowed upon "the chosen ones" by generations of healers before them to study and learn the arts of herbal medicine, healing, mind-reading, birthing, and the mysteries of the supernatural. It is my duty and honour to mentor you in this pursuit for a period of eight years, for the good of all our people, as your mother is not here to do so.

Matilda arose from her bed that very day a changed woman. She now had a purpose, beyond that of being the King's wife, which raised her spirits in both an anxious and exciting way. She shared her aunt's prophesy and "calling" with her husband, King Edwin; he went from skepticism to shock to hope, and then to glee. He was overjoyed at seeing the delight back in his wife's sparkling green eyes. The king was willing to believe just about anything to not only have his true love back by his side, but to finally have hope that a child of their own would one day replace him on the throne. If this meant having his lunatic sister-in-law back in their lives, so be it, though his advisors would be adamantly against Elizabeth's return and his wife's new vocation. Some within his realm believed being "different" meant being evil and ungodly. He, therefore, decided to keep her "medicinal" training a secret within the castle walls.

Queen Matilda studied under the tutelage of her aunt well beyond the eight years she'd promised to prepare for the coming of her daughter. She discovered how little she knew of life beyond the walls of the palace, but kept her heart and mind open in order to understand and support those she ruled. Queen Matilda dedicated her entire being to serving the kingdom by her husband's side, as well as becoming a gifted seer like her Aunt Elizabeth. As time went on, gossip spread of her miraculous healing abilities and eventually, both rich and poor began to seek her council. At her husband and aunt's insistence, she disguised herself in peasant clothes as she entered the various villages when called upon. She was never left defenseless outside the castle walls thanks to the king's guardsmen who were ordered to support and protect their queen at all costs.

The king shared a secret of his own with his beloved. For centuries, the magical gift of communicating with all the animals in the land had been bestowed upon the monarchy, unbeknownst to the kingdom's subjects, of course. This fascinating reveal opened up a portal of intimacy between the couple bringing them even closer.

Queen Matilda anointed the sick and the dying, and she healed the lame, sad, fevered and diseased. She also helped birth many infants, and thus became known as "The Queen of Grace," among her people. Through her work she realized all beings were born equal in the eyes of God, even though their circumstances varied. The more she lived out her purpose, the more Matilda realized that most people bled the same, loved the same, mourned the same, and died the same.

Satisfaction and joy were the by-products of using the power of her heart and hands in her life's work, that is, until she turned forty-years-old and her Aunt Elizabeth's vision of long ago came true. On that blessed day, a love beyond anything Queen Matilda had ever know set up camp in her heart for life, as the midwife laid baby Maya in her arms for the first time. Folding back the ivory lace coverlet, she kissed her baby's forehead, inhaled her precious scent, and whispered, "You will rule the kingdom one day, my child." Then she gently handed her back into the arms of an attendant.

Queen Mya became a wise woman, a diviner, a clairvoyant, a healer, and a sage according to the prophecy, and administered to her royal subjects for the duration of her reign. Her mother, Queen Matilda, continued to advise and guide her daughter on all matters, both personal and professional, until she left this world for a better one at the age of seventy-two.

The farmer, his wife, and the members of his family became loyal servants of the court, discovering the truth about their young wards years later. Their life of toil and strife was over, thanks to divine providence and a new way of looking at life. Mya passed along the eight life principles and the reams of wisdom she'd learned from her mother, Queen Matilda. She also told the family that what people focused on said, "This is what I want the most," and the Great Beyond would land it in their lap—good or otherwise. In thanks for the part this family had played in her training, Queen Maya had a lovely cottage built for them, educated the children, found honourable positions for the older ones, and made sure the family never wanted for anything until they left this world. In turn, the farmer, his wife, and their children passed her sage advice along to other villagers, acknowledging the miraculous change of circumstances that had been bestowed upon them all.

Queen Mya's cousin and best friend, Roberta, fell in love with Lord Geoffery Howard, and bore two children—a girl and a boy— Francesca and William. The couple lived within the castle, serving her Royal Highness in myriad capacities with devotion and love.

Throughout the kingdom, the new queen was cherished and adored for the reverence she bestowed upon all living things, thanks to her upbringing. Her mother, Queen Matilda, encouraged her to see life through her heart, not her eyes. Mya had been raised from a young age to practice remembering who she was as she'd been instructed, with fortitude, mercy and generosity of matter and spirit. She frequently called upon her animal friends for help, guidance and reassurance. The eight principles of life, and the deeply ingrained wisdom passed down to her, was taught to every man, woman, and child under her rule. Her goodness was reflected in the hearts, minds and deeds of her people. Mya, like her mother, not only became skilled in the healing arts and supernatural wisdom, but also educated other women called to this work. Educating her people in reading, writing, higher morals, business, justice, and hygiene was paramount to Mya so they could live better lives. This set the foundation for prosperity and growth and yes, peace, throughout the land.

Her Highness, Queen Mya, chose not to take a husband, despite a number of marriage proposals over the years. When asked, she always replied, "I am married to my people ... I am devoted to them and they to me. Raising the quality of the lives for which I am responsible, and fulfilling my sovereign duties IS my life. That, for me, is enough."

Princess Francesca, the first-born child of Queen Mya's cousin, Roberta, and her husband, Geoffrey, was chosen by Queen Mya herself to succeed her on the throne. Though Roberta was never called to the life of healing and magic, her daughter, Francesca, had a natural inborn affinity to it, and took to it like bees to honey. Queen Mya saw to her training from the age of ten until she was skilled enough to fly on her own.

Queen Mya led the thriving realm until her peaceful death in her ninety-fifth year. Etched on the wall of the mausoleum above her tomb was written, "Remember Who You Are" and inlaid beneath these words was a stone with the number eight engraved on it. It was the simple, yet profound gift her mother, Queen Matilda, had placed in her hand many years earlier as a reminder to always remember who she was—a divine child of God, born with gifts and talents worthy of creating a new legacy, lasting change, and magic in the world.

THE END

What Have I Learned?

Breadcrumbs Gathered on My Planetary Picnic

As I twist-tie Eat Your Crusts to a close, I have a big goofy, self-satisfied smile plastered on my kisser. I want to thank you for taking the time to read my book. Before starting this journey, I was informed by many writers and editors that it took great courage to write a book and they weren't lying. There were a bunch of stories I had written previously and thrown into a one-day, some-day file until I was confronted with the cancer diagnosis. Well, that certainly lit a fire under my ass to get a move on with this book. It was challenging and scary, as well as life-affirming. I am so proud of the gumption and strength within me for pulling this off. I loved the whole process, except the tech crap, and I've learned a lot. Sitting down and revisiting my stories led to sobbing my face off, then giving thanks for my sweet life—my wonderful parents who taught me plenty, my five amazing, hilarious, idiotic brothers, my loving, kind, handsome-bastard husband, and all our family and friends.

My quest for understanding what makes us tick, on a deeper level, began with a lot of head-scratching at the age of twenty-three. I signed up for a meditation class in Toronto provided by Eli Bay called, "The Relaxation Response," which I thought might be a good place to start for a newbie. I attended these classes after work for three months, and I was hooked on "going within." After that, I joined a yoga studio closer to home; it was the whole meal-deal—mental, physical, and spiritual practices that aimed to quiet the mind from a detached witness state (observing the thoughts flitting in, out, and around the grey matter, a situation often referred to as monkey-mind). To my delight, it relieved stress, promoted relaxation, and made me more aware of an inner world, beyond our thoughts, and its significance in our lives. My body's always been flexible, so the yoga postures were easy and fun for me, though the

166

balancing poses could be a bitch. Post-posturing, we would sing and chant mantras or meditate, which put some of the participants into an altered state of consciousness, beyond the ego's relentless yammering, and into the Present or Now moment. I was not one of the ones who had a mind-blowing experience, and sometimes I thought some of this stuff was woo-woo, but I wanted to up my experience, and it set me on a forward trajectory.

Thus began my hunger to know more about the conscious, sub-conscious, and super-conscious mind, so I decided to jump down that rabbit hole. I wanted to learn how to reset my frazzled nervous system, heal what was unbalanced and hurting inside, as well as understand the science behind why we are here, while discovering the highest version of myself. I'd struggled with digestive, menstrual, and anxiety issues since my early twenties and this was the catalyst to my search for healing, both inside and out. We are much more than what we think we are, and miracles are truly possible. I know this because I've witnessed some amazing ones. Deepening the connection with myself was my numero-uno priority. This is not one-stop shopping by any means; it is a practice that I'll harness and hone for the rest of my life.

Like a starving kid after school, I couldn't get enough reading in whatever called to me in the areas of science—notably, quantum physics—as well as spirituality, conscious evolution, and healing. My mom used to say if I was hungry, I should have a piece of bread and butter before dinner. Yeck! I wanted substance, baby, something that really filled me up and satisfied me!

One of the first books I read in my early twenties was a memoir called *Man's Search for Meaning* by Viktor Frankel, an Austrian psychiatrist. Dr. Frankl chronicled his experiences from 1942 to 1945 as a prisoner in four different concentration camps during World War II, his last being in the Nazi concentration camp, Auschwitz. In this hell-hole he lost his parents, brother, and pregnant wife. Dr. Frankl observed that those of his fellow inmates who survived were able to connect with a purpose in life they could feel positive about—such as conversing with an (imagined) loved one—and then they immersed themselves in imagining that purpose.

According to Frankl, the way a prisoner imagined the future affected their longevity. From this fascinating read I learned valuable lessons in physical and spiritual survival when we are faced with the most horrific circumstances. A simple summary is that he taught his readers that we cannot avoid suffering, but we can choose how to accept and endure through the most dire of circumstances, find meaning in them, and move forward with renewed purpose. I gleaned from Mr. Frankl's wise words that the meaning of life is found in every precious moment, even in suffering and death. It's all about the choices we make even in the most dreadful circumstances. Tibetans have a similar saying, "Change is inevitable, suffering is optional." I recall Dr. Frankl noting,

"I had been convinced that there were certain things I just could not do: I could not sleep without this or I could not live with that or the other. The first night in Auschwitz, we slept in beds which were constructed in tiers. On each tier (measuring about six-and-a-half to eight feet) slept nine men, directly on the boards. Two blankets were shared by nine men. We could, of course lie only on our sides crowded and huddled against each other, which had some advantage because of the bitter cold. Light sleepers, who used to be disturbed by the slightest noise in the next room now found themselves pressed against a comrade who snored loudly a few inches from his ear and yet slept quite soundly through the noise."[2]

When I first read this story, I realized how many of my entrenched beliefs such as, "I can only sleep in total silence and darkness, with lots of warm blankies, two feather pillows, and a heat bag," would have been thrown out the window, had I been faced with a situation such as this. Frankl wrote, "Everything can

---

[2] Viktor Frankl, *Man's Search for Meaning* (Boston, Massachusetts: Beacon Press, 2006), Pages 17-18.

be taken from a man but one thing: the last human freedoms—to choose one's attitude in any given set of circumstances and to choose one's own way."

Sickness, pain, emotional disorders, depression, anxiety, unhappiness, and exhaustion are more often than not due to repressed or suppressed emotions that reside within us that lead to limited beliefs, programming, patterns, and behaviour. Simply said, our inner world reflects our outer world. When we can become aware of, acknowledge, surrender, and release these heavy emo-tions, which are often buried deep within our psyche since child-hood, we'll create more peace, harmony, and flow within ourselves and in this world. Sounds easy, right? Yah ... uh huh. Remember, the true essence of you is not controlled by your circumstances or by what others think of you.

Here are a few things I practice when I feel out-of-sorts, cranky, anxious, afraid, lost, pissy, threatened, or defensive—which hap-pens on a regular basis, let me tell ya'. Hey, I'm human!

First off, I ask myself: What's showing up right NOW?

This is when I enter my quiet space (silence) and meet what is demanding my attention in terms of thoughts, emotions, or physical sensations. Often, the little Lois inside of me is feeling unsafe or afraid. There are so many programs and patterns within me that try their damnedest to guard me against being threatened, hurt, ridiculed, criticized, judged, abandoned, controlled, or dismissed all over again.

Obsessing over things, judging, gossiping, defending, censoring, attacking, manipulating, and proving how worthy and wonderful we are sucks us dry and leaves us depleted.

I have learned that beneath every uncomfortable emotion is usually fear or shame. Resisting these and other feelings such as anger, hurt, loneliness, frustration, rage, and sadness, or suppress-ing them further, leads to stress, pain, anger, depression, anxiety, and illness, as I mentioned earlier. When this shit comes up, I let it be okay and welcome it. It's not always easy, but the more you practice, the better you feel. This is not the time to figure it out or analyze the crap out of it. Feel the feeling, then go within and see where this emotion is residing within your body and give it permission to be there—e.g., "I'm allowed to feel anger in my chest." We try to control things and resist what is showing up so we don't have to face our fear. Like a two-year-old's temper, it needs to be felt, expressed, and released, which diffuses the energy of these powerful emotions. If we continue to fight, resist or try to fix our problems, then we're still at the same frequency with what we're at war with – perfectionism, proving ourselves, being good enough, etc. "Level-up" in all that you do; move into love, acceptance, compassion, and forgiveness for yourself and others.

These days we increasingly read that stress leads to increased inflammation in the body and puts the nervous system into hyperoverdrive (Flight, Fight, Freeze). This state of being is out of alignment with who we really are, our true Self. When I become aware of excess tension in my body—neck/shoulders/gut—or my breathing becomes shallow, or I experience anxious or angry thoughts, I have to remind myself to let go of the constant chasing, obsessing, defending, analyzing, complaining, judging, grasping, controlling, desperation, fixing, and seeking *(what do I do to make this go away? I have to figure this out/fix this!)*. These parts of my personality stem mostly from childhood, and I created them out of fear in order to protect myself from abuse, anger, and criticism, and to shield myself from the possibility people might not like or approve of me. These programs within our subconscious mind love to run the show; they're simply on autopilot in Survivalville. This is all-consuming and creates havoc both inside and outside of us. It also creates opportunities for us to listen to the wise voice inside that has our back at all times. When you stop chasing whatever it is you so fervently want, (the ideal partner, job, body, health, house, bank account, status, or perfection), exciting things start coming to you. We think that when we get this thing, we'll be happy. When this "thing" doesn't happen, we get all freaked out. A new way of thinking can be, "When I'm accepting and ok with what's showing up, things will open up, and that's when the fun begins: miracles, synchronicities, and surprises show up.

I ask myself: *What am I putting out there in the world? Is it: poor me (victim), I'm broken and need fixing, I'm invisible, something is wrong, I'm not safe, I'm not good enough, I have to be perfect/right/careful/in control, or I'll never be happy unless "such and such" happens. Am I that kinda person?* Have you heard the expression, "The mind makes a wonderful servant, but a terrible master," by Robin Sharma, the author of *The Monk Who Sold His Ferrari?*[3] It's a good one.

Life responds to everything we make up in our heads around what should and shouldn't happen (our repetitive thoughts) from day to day. If you approach life from "I am broken and need fixing," you will find things that are broken and need fixing. If you believe you're not a lovable human being, you will attract people in your life that reflect this very belief. When you continue to focus on something, like, "I'll never find a soul mate" and then collect evidence that it's true, it becomes a reality, because the Universe always assumes it's what you want more of.

I also ask myself:

a) What am I becoming and what do I want to experience? and

b) What's totally possible in my life?"

This is an exercise in seeing and feeling your future now. You have to align to the frequency of these desires. This is quantum physics, baby! The Universe responds to the Present moment/Now, and it is the gateway to higher awareness. This is where meditation, journaling, and breathwork come in handy. It is how this book came to be.

I begin by writing down what I envision for my future life in a journal, no matter what my current reality looks like. Recording

---

[3] Robin Sharma, The Monk Who Sold His Ferrari, (New York: Harper Collins, 1999), p. 51.

evidence that the higher realms are working on my behalf is fun and gets my juices flowing. Aim high, then even higher in your dreams and desires. You must let your expectations go and let Life Force work its magic. The answers and solutions show up when you let go of control.

Here is a personal example of the "envisioning my future" exercise that I wrote six months before I began writing this book. It read: *I am over the moon at what a kick-ass writer and author I have become. I have surpassed anything I could ever have dreamed of. It has taken me places I never imagined, and raised my creativity and confidence to new heights. Fulfilling and elated doesn't begin to describe this whole birthing process. The delivery wasn't easy, but well worth the pain. I am one powerful, brave, gutsy gal.*

The result of this imagining in my mind is currently sitting in your hands.

This is an inside job—no one can do it for you! It's all about your energetic frequency. Your vision must be bigger than your fear, doubt, dread, old habits, and excuses about why you can't experience what you desire. You can only transcend the ego's fears, shame, blame, and guilt with Love. This expanded vision of your life surpasses all the darkness, heaviness, and pain you've been schlepping around for decades.

Beyond our deepest fears, insecurities, outdated beliefs, limiting patterns, and programs (held deep within our subconscious mind) is a greater consciousness called God, Universal Intelligence, Higher Wisdom, Life Force, the Great Beyond, ... call it what you will. It's about Freedom, Light, and Love—true liberation. Accept, allow, surrender, and feel what you are trying to wrestle to the ground—your emotions, pain, a diagnosis, relationships, parenting, finances, and so on. Through adversity we are always being called to our Highest Self. It can be a roller-coaster ride, a shit show, or an eye-opening experience, and often all of the above. You may have to feel through your biggest fears—sickness, death, failure, shame, loss, loneliness, abandonment, unworthiness, not-good-enoughs, being unlovable, and financial loss, to name a few. We all have them. They lie deep within our subconscious mind, and love to sit in the driver's seat and navigate our course.

My body is always working on my behalf and not—as I believed for years—against me. Connect with the sensations in your body with love and compassion. Ask them what they want or need, and if they have something to share with you. Everything that shows up in our lives is a mirror to the unseen patterns and programming in our mind and body—again, the inner world mirrors the outer world. It bears repeating.

Higher consciousness is always calling us to go beyond the fears that keep us small, safe, in our comfort zone, stuck, censored, contracted, or conforming to rules of society, family, religion, race, and nationality. It's not about doing more, figuring out what's wrong and trying to fix it, or trying to escape what you fear the most. We become addicted to these ways of being, but once we realize we keep falling into the same pothole, we can then choose whether or not we want to stay in the same old, same old. Take your power back by doing things that are nurturing and energizing, and that make you feel good, rather than things that add even more pressure and stress to your life. Sounds pretty easy, huh? Let me tell you, it takes practice every single day of your life.

Your True Self isn't a loud-mouth Lucy, its voice is gentle, patient, and persistent, and it encourages you to move both forward and deep. Deep as in feeling those parts of you that you want to bury and hide. Those parts of you just don't want to be hurt again.

Want to feel better? Judge less! This takes dedication and yes, that word again, practice—lots of it. We are all definitely works in progress as it is so ingrained within us to look for what's wrong rather than what's right—what life *should* be rather than what it is. Just witness a dinner party these days. What are the topics of discussion? ... politics, war, crime, health woes, and the state of the world. There are a lot of "Debbie Downers" out there. We, as a race, are voracious judgey-McJudgers, which often hurts us more than who or what we are judging. Falling into this trap is so common because we've witnessed and learned to judge (good/bad, right/wrong) from a young age. It's a natural thing for the ego to do, but when it becomes a nasty habit, it causes damage both inside and out.

These days I am getting clearer in my desire for the grit, the shit, the fight, the might, the real and the feel of open, honest, and real conversations. I am not interested in the benign, "I'm fine," boring, ho-hum, dart-n-dash-for-safety, bullshit conversations anymore. Lamenting over the state of the world isn't going to change it. I believe we all hold the power to change it for the better, and it begins with each and every one of us taking responsibility for our own inner world. A true warrior, they say, is about vulnerability. So, this is my contribution.

Here's something else I do:

First thing in the morning and before I go to bed, I ask myself, "Who would I be, act like, feel like, and present to the world if I had nothing holding me back? What is my heart calling for? Let these questions sit, percolate, and gain potency. I invite you to record them in a journal by your bed. I also make a list in my head of all the things I am grateful for as well as appreciate in my life. Then I place my hand on my heart and recall a time in my life when I felt immense love and joy. I breathe this feeling into my heart space and wait until I feel the lovefest deep within my core. Yep, sounds kinda koo koo, but it works.

I have just passed through the arrival gate of my last trimester and what I know for dang sure is that I have learned a lot. But the more I know, the more I realize I don't know. I am both scared and excited (scarecited) to see not only where I am heading, but where the topics of mind-body healthcare, technology, human consciousness, religion, quantum physics, and global change are moving the evolution of humanity towards in the future. The adventure continues ...

There's only one you; nobody can do you, but you. Mine the blessed bits that make you, *you* and share the gifts that make your soul sing at the top of its lungs with the world. I also highly recom-mend you do the things that challenge you the most. That's when you feel the most alive, (i.e., write a book, take a course, get up on stage, dare yourself to sing Karaoke, learn to—sail, play tennis, swim, cook/blog/knit/paint, do Jiu-Jitsu, volunteer, become a photographer ...)

The best advice my mother gave me was to always make time for your friends. This takes time, devotion and care, but they are the ones who will pull you through the kick-me-in-the-ass times in your life. I love and adore these besties of mine who lift me up when I'm down, make me snort tea through my nose from laughing so hard, love me to bits, and inspire and encourage me in all my creative endeavours. Thank you to Valerie, Mary, Fran, Leslie, Carla, Caron, Monique, Jennifer, Lori, Lela, Patricia, Ann Marie, Melanie, Kim, Lela, Mar Mar, Sandy, and Lizzie, who are my "chamomile tea, a good book, double-dipped DQ ice cream cone, bag of Lays and sensational pair of boots" gal-pals for life. In other words, the loves of my life. All my friends over the years, near and far, mean the world to me and I am so grateful our happy, perfectly timed connection aligned along the way. With every friendship I've had has come an armful of gifts, laughter, lessons, and wisdom.

Another pearl I have come to rely on is the ability and strength to say "no" when I mean and feel it viscerally. Pay close attention to those yappy guilt-ridden "I should, I can't say no, I owe them, I feel responsible for them, what if they don't like me anymore, I'll be judged, I'm obligated" voices. Listening to my heart's first instinct builds my intuition's muscle. I think we could all use a personal trainer in this weight-bearing exercise on a moment-to-moment basis.

Life is learning, and this is so important in asking for what you want versus what you don't want, because it's imperative to our happiness. For example, I wanted more quality time with my husband, John, so I suggested to him we turn off the television and eat dinner at the table. He looked at me like I just said I'd sold his precious golf clubs. I swear his chin quivered. Notice I didn't say, "I want us to talk more; share our feelings." Nope, most men go squirrelly when you bring up this subject, and I didn't want him running for the hills.

This is new territory for us as we've eaten in front of the TV every night since we've been married—which was a long time ago.

I've read that you have to ask clearly and specifically for what you want and do it from your heart. "If you don't ask, you don't get" is one of my all-time fave quotes, which I use regularly. It went like this: "I want to spend more quality time with you. Can we turn off the television while we eat?" Changing things up often starts with baby-step actions. I compromised, so when we have lunch at home together, we do so in telecommunication-technology silence, allowing time for more intimate discussions. Thinking in a new way can produce different results. It's very easy to fall back into old habits, to be sure, but I think the trick is to be mindful of the choices we make. I love that saying if you want something different to happen you have to change the way you think and act to get the results you want. Once again, bears repeating.

The expression, "dry toast" could never be used to describe this life of mine; an ideal reason to write and share *Eat Your Crusts* with you, my dear readers. No matter how you slice it, aren't we all part of a big ol' family here on this cosmic orb we call home? Some of these family members you adore and others ... meh, not so much. What we do have in common is we're all basically the same, deep down, and feel the same feelings, but with different stories. What we see in another person is also a part of ourselves.

My calling as I go forward is to free myself from the hold the past can have over me, as well as curtail the habit of worry, the what ifs, and obsessive planning of my future. Why? To find the soft, gushy, pliable centre—just like that slice of bread we talked about at the beginning of this book—where peace, calm, and serenity lie, if only for a sweet spell every day. Practicing being in the Now Moment will make you a more centred, grounded person.

I mentioned holotropic breathwork previously, and I love it so much, I will mention it again. It's a tool I implement regularly to quiet the heavy traffic between my ears and connect to myself on a deeper level. This stuff is amazing! "Riding the breath," is like a bridge that brings you beyond the thinking mind, or the mental narrative, to what is referred to as, "the sweet spot, still-point, silence in the Now moment, or emptiness." Whatever you want to call it, it is a temporary surrendering of the ego as you feel into your truth and authenticity. Breathwork moves us to a space where our tendency to think, control, fix, plan, judge, doubt, and solve gets to take a load off and leave us in a space of peace. Breathwork has been around for centuries, but is fairly new to the Western world. Not only is breathwork able to put you into altered states of consciousness, but is one of the easiest ways to release suppressed emotions without having to do talk therapy, which can be arduous and unsuccessful for many. The first time I practised this with my friend, Susan S., I was in awe with how raw and real the emotional pain came up, seemingly out of nowhere and attached to no-thing. I had a great heaving bawl for a minute or two, and poof, it was over and I commenced connecting to my breath. I was hooked! Who knows how much stored shit lies in the deep dark passages of our soul? The benefits of deep breathing are many—it regulates the nervous system, increases oxygen to all the cells, boosts mood and immunity, increases energy, focus, and memory, promotes quality sleep, as well as reducing symptoms of anxiety, depression, and stress. When we breathe deeply, we expand our life force.

Using art, writing, and somatic dance, I am a leader in creative self-expression for women hell bent on knowing and showing themselves, unapologetically, in a community called, "Gather The Women." By offering a safe and loving environment to wake up, shake up, open up and speak up, I am doing my part in creating healthier, happier, more confidently expressed women.

And last but not least, thank you for sharing precious time and space with me on this planet. May we all do our part in bringing more love, acceptance, understanding, liberation, and peace not only to ourselves but to all who live in this troubled but magnificent world as well. So let it be said, so let it be done. Shaboom. Shaboom.

From my heart to yours, thank you again for reading my book. I love you,

Lois

Back of the Book Prayer

This prayer from my Lutheran upbringing was recited verbatim every night before bed during my early childhood:

Now I lay me down to sleep
I pray the Lord my soul to keep
If I should die before I wake
I pray thee Lord, my soul to take.
God bless Mommy and Daddy, all my sweet brothers, Grandma and Grandpa Penhale, all my sweet aunts, all my sweet uncles, and all my sweet cousins.
Please help me to be a good girl.
Amen.

New updated version

As I hunker down to rest
I pray, oh Lord, eight hours at best
If I should awaken to another day
Oh, joy, oh bliss, hip, hip, hooray!

God bless my Johnny, so sweet and so kind
All my five brothers, I'm so glad they're mine.
To those who took an early flight,
Get down and boogie in the love and the light
Bless those friends, so dear to my heart,
I'll love you forever, never to part.
Please help me to be the miracle you see,
Precious, perfect, unlimited, and free.

The Guest House

This being human is a guest house;
Every morning a new arrival.
A joy, a depression, a meanness,
some momentary awareness comes
as an unexpected visitor.

Welcome and entertain them all,
even if they're a crowd of sorrows
who violently sweep your house
empty of its furniture.

Still, treat each guest honourably.
He may be clearing you out
For some new delight.

The dark thought, the shame, the malice.
Meet them at the door laughing
and invite them in.

Be grateful for whatever comes
Because each has been sent
As a guide from beyond.

Rumi, Sufi Poet, the 1200s

Acknowledgements

M any thanks to those who inspired and encouraged me at the beginning of this wild ride into the creative writing world to find my own voice and put it down on paper—Aprille Janes and the Tuesday afternoon writing group, Jaclyn Desforges and Sue Reynolds.

It takes a village, so gobs of gratitude go to...the beta readers team—Raissa, Caron, Carla, and Valerie, for bringing their strengths and talents to the table in order for my own to shine, ... my editor, Susan Crossman of Crossman Communications, for her heart, soul, and dedication to her craft, as well as the generosity of time and patience she extended to me during this book writing process, ... Sue Reynolds of the publishing team, Stones Throw Publishing, who assisted in assembling all the ingredients to turn out this book, ... Anne Hampson, my creativity and life coach, and ... Cindy, Nicky, Diana M., and Johnny, my techno-team ... a whopping thank you to Sue Stirling for the great fun in coming up with the "head and body shots" for this book ... and finally, Monique L. and Carla Z. who took me by the hand and walked—okay, dragged—me through the deep, dark and delicious direct marketing hallways.

To my dear friends and family who mean the world to me. Some may not always understand this curious creative process, but you are always there to cheerlead me on.

A special shout-out to my dear friend, Judith, saying, "I did it!" I know she would be thrilled for me, having been an author herself. She decided to take an early flight to the celestial "all-inclusive" so she could fly free. Love and miss you, Jude.

To my beloved husband, John, who is my oak tree, standing firm and rooted in his devotion and love for me so I can test my wings on whatever wackadoodle adventure I am currently embarking on. Thank you for this life we have.

Bibliography

The following are books, authors and speakers whose work has, in many ways, fed my soul, moved me forward, and quenched my thirst for knowledge.

Brown, Michael. *The Presence Process*, published in Vancouver, Canada by Namaste Publishing in 2010.

Ferry, Matthew. *Quiet Mind, Epic Life: Escape the Status Quo and Experience Enlightened Prosperity Now*, United States, Independently published in 2018.

Frankl, Viktor E., *Man's Search For Meaning*, published in Boston, Massachusetts by Beacon Press in 2006. Originally published in 1946.

Hough, Jennifer. *Unstuck: The Physics of Getting Out Of Your Own Way*, published in Asheville, North Carolina by I Fly Publishing in 2022.

Lipton, Bruce H. *The Biology of Belief: Unleashing the Power of Consciousness, Matter, and Miracles*, published in the United States by Hay House Inc. in 2005.

McTaggart, Lynne, *The Field: The Quest For The Secret Force Of The Universe*, published in the United States by HarperCollins in 2002.

Moorjani, Anita. *Dying To Be Me*, published in the United States by Hay House Inc. in 2012.

Parkin, John C. *Fuck It: The Ultimate Spiritual Way*, published in the United States by Hay House Inc. in 2010.

Sharma, Robin S. *The Monk Who Sold His Ferrari: A Fable About Fulfilling Your Dreams and Reaching Your Destiny*, published in the United States by HarperCollins in 1999.

Sullivan, Dan. *The Gap And The Gain: The High Achiever's Guide to Happiness, Confidence, and Success*, published in the United States by Hay House Inc. in 2021.

Tolle, Eckhart. *A New Earth: Awakening To Your Life's Purpose*, published in the United States by Hay House Inc. in 2005.

Any works by Gregg Braden, Brene Brown, Kyle Cease, Pema Chodron, Dr. Joe Dispenza, Glennon Doyle, David Hawkins, or Rupert Spira.

About the Author

Lois Howard Lenarduzzi moseyed into the art world quite by accident. Due to health issues, she gave up her massage therapy practice and began a journey back to herself through the arts of creative self-expression—writing, dance, painting, drumming, and singing. She continues to find new ways to truly know and show herself, which can be terrifying but also liberating in these trying times of change. Lois believes that honouring her callings continues to open the creative portal to the bigger, bolder, and more beautiful in her life.

Lois currently lives in Ancaster, Ontario, with her husband, John.

How To Connect and Work with Lois

Lois offers creative writing classes/workshops, somatic dance classes, and creative self-expression workshops (which can include writing, somatic dance, breathwork, meditation, journaling and painting). She also hosts GATHER THE WOMEN community circles in the Hamilton area. Lois is also available for speaking engagements.

Contact Lois if...

You are struggling to move forward on the creative path and/or wish to explore the creative part of you that is begging and screaming for some self-expression—through writing, painting, somatic dance, journaling, and breathwork. Exercising your creativity opens you up to many gifts and surprises ... like uncovering parts of you that have been holding you back from being who you came here to be, taking more risks, becoming more powerful and secure in how you present yourself to the world.

You want to be a part of the GATHER THE WOMEN community, where you are called to Remember Who You Are—that is, becoming the best and brightest versions of yourself using the arts of self-expression: creative writing, somatic dance, breathwork, journaling, and meditation. Many of us are afraid to show or express our true selves by hiding secrets, pretending, censoring, conforming, people-pleasing, or playing small and safe. In this group setting, you're encouraged to be honest, open, and vulnerable as we explore, discover and play. You may just discover programs and patterns held deep within the subconscious mind (often associated with fear, anger, shame, and guilt) that have kept you stuck in the past, holding you back from realizing your true power, gifts, and purpose. In the GATHER THE WOMEN community, we honour each member's story in a safe, caring environment to wake up, shake up, open up, and speak up, which creates a portal to expanded awareness, creativity, and an enhanced body, mind, and spirit.

This was the impetus for me to write this book, *Eat Your Crusts*. I promised myself to stop playing safe and small, and hiding what made me uncomfortable to share. This was a gift to myself to celebrate how far I have come (and how much further I will go) to open

185

up that portal to the bigger, bolder, and more beautiful that awaits me.

Contact the author, Lois Howard Lenarduzzi,
via email at itsaduzzi8@gmail.com
and on Facebook, Messenger, and Instagram.